Morris GRAVES: Blind Bird. 1940. Gouache, 30⅛ x 27". The Museum of Modern Art, New York.

Romantic Painting in America

by James Thrall Soby and Dorothy C. Miller

The Museum of Modern Art, New York

Reprint Edition, 1969
Published for The Museum of Modern Art by Arno Press

Reprint Edition, 1969 Arno Press Library of Congress Catalog Card No. 73-86430

Contents

Foreword and Acknowledgment

The exhibition which accompanies this book presents the Romantic spirit in American painting as a persistent tendency beginning in the late 18th century and continuing with the youngest painters of today. While the exhibition does not attempt a complete survey, it does explore a wide range of American Romantic art, some of it long neglected or viewed heretofore in another light, some too recent to be generally known. The Romantic tradition emerges as one of the strong and continuous currents in American painting.

Wartime restrictions and various other factors have made it impossible to borrow certain paintings of capital importance to an exhibition of American Romantic art. Notable among these are Trumbull's *Battle of Bunker's Hill*, Allston's *Moonlit Landscape*, Morse's *Allegorical Landscape with New York University*, several major works by Thomas Cole including *The Course of Empire* series, Ryder's *Jonah, The Flying Dutchman, Siegfried* and *The Race Track*, Homer's *Summer Night* and *The Life Line*. In the contemporary field a number of painters whose work might have been appropriate to the exhibition could not be represented because of limitations of space.

On behalf of the President and Trustees of the Museum of Modern Art the director of the exhibition wishes to thank the collectors, institutions and dealers whose generosity in lending has made the exhibition possible. In addition, grateful acknowledgment is made to the following for assistance in securing loans and for many valuable suggestions: C. G. Abbot; Jere Abbott; Mrs. H. D. Allen; A. Everett Austin, Jr.; John I. H. Baur; Donald J. Bear; Mrs. Florence Paull Berger; T. E. Blackwell; Miss Louise H. Burchfield; Clyde H. Burroughs; Charles D. Childs; W. G. Constable; Henry Wadsworth Longfellow Dana; Miss Louisa Dresser; Carleton V. Earle; G. H. Edgell; David E. Finley; Mrs. Juliana Force; Joseph T. Fraser, Jr.; Blake-More Godwin; Lloyd Goodrich; William A. Gosline, Jr.; J. D. Hatch, Jr.; Dalzell Hatfield; Bartlett H. Hayes, Jr.; Arthur W. Heintzelman; Horace H. F. Jayne; Fiske Kimball; Marchal E. Landgren; Clifford L. Lord; Robert G. McIntyre; Henri Marceau; Frank Jewett Mather, Jr.; Miss Agnes Mongan; Mrs. Gertrude H. Moore; Dr. Grace L. McCann Morley; Charles Nagel, Jr.; Harry Shaw Newman; John O'Connor, Jr.; Duncan Phillips; Reginald Poland; Paul North Rice; Daniel Catton Rich; E. P. Richardson; Mrs. Isabel S. Roberts; Paul J. Sachs; Charles H. Sawyer; Edgar C. Schenck; Mrs. Alice M. Sharkey; Benjamin H. Stone; Frederick A. Sweet; Francis Henry Taylor; Ruel P. Tolman; W. R. Valentiner; Harry B. Wehle; Dr. Alexander Wetmore; Mrs. Harriet Whedon; Miss Beatrice Winser; Miss Ella Winter. Of the Museum staff, Elise Van Hook and William S. Lieberman have contributed special research.

DOROTHY C. MILLER, *Director of the Exhibition*

Lenders to the Exhibition

Mr. and Mrs. Frederick B. Adams, Jr., New York; Matthew Barnes, San Francisco; Lt. and Mrs. Alastair Bradley-Martin, Glen Head, N. Y.; Stephen C. Clark, New York; Mr. and Mrs. I. M. Cohen, New York; Mrs. Algernon Coolidge, Boston; Henry Wadsworth Longfellow Dana, Cambridge, Mass.; Mrs. Louise M. Dunn, Cleveland; Philip L. Goodwin, New York; A. Conger Goodyear, Old Westbury; Mr. and Mrs. Buell Hammett, Santa Barbara; Miss Anna Warren Ingersoll, Penllyn, Pa.; Mrs. Sheldon Keck, Brooklyn; Vance Kirkland, Denver; Rico Lebrun, Westport, Conn.; The Lewisohn Collection, New York; Mr. and Mrs. Milton Lowenthal, New York; Lt. Edward Millman, New York; Paul Mommer, New York; Mrs. Leighton K. Montgomery, Brooklyn; Frank C. Osborn, Manchester, Vt.; Harry T. Peters, New York; Alton Pickens, New York; Theodore C. Polos, San Francisco; David Porter, Washington; Mr. and Mrs. Bernard Reis, New York; Ernest Rosenfeld, New York; Lt. and Mrs. Bruce Ryan, New York; John L. Sexton, Wilmington; Nat Sharfman, Boston; George L. Shaskan, Poundridge, N. Y.; Mrs. Otto L. Spaeth, Dayton; Pfc. Boetius H. Sullivan, Jr., Chicago; Mark Tobey, Seattle; Curt Valentin, New York; Mrs. Payne Whitney, New York; Miss Denny Winters, Los Angeles.

Addison Gallery of American Art, Phillips Academy, Andover; Museum of Fine Arts, Boston; Public Library of the City of Boston; Art Institute of Chicago; Cincinnati Art Museum; New York State Historical Association, Cooperstown; Detroit Institute of Arts; Wadsworth Atheneum, Hartford; Honolulu Academy of Arts; Newark Museum; Brooklyn Museum, New York; Metropolitan Museum of Art, New York; New York Public Library; Whitney Museum of American Art, New York; Smith College Museum of Art, Northampton; Pennsylvania Academy of the Fine Arts, Philadelphia; Philadelphia Museum of Art; Museum of Historic Art, Princeton University; Rochester Memorial Art Gallery; Washington University, St. Louis; Fine Arts Society, San Diego; Toledo Museum of Art; National Collection of Fine Arts, Washington; United States National Museum, Washington; Phillips Memorial Gallery, Washington; Worcester Art Museum.

A.C.A. Gallery; H. V. Allison & Co.; An American Place; Associated American Artists; Buchholz Gallery; Contemporary Arts; Downtown Gallery; Durlacher Brothers; Kennedy & Co.; Kleemann Galleries; M. Knoedler & Co.; Kraushaar Galleries; Julien Levy Gallery; Macbeth Gallery; Pierre Matisse Gallery; Midtown Galleries; Milch Galleries; A. F. Mondschein; J. B. Neumann; The Old Print Shop; Passedoit Gallery; Perls Galleries; Frank K. M. Rehn Gallery; Victor D. Spark; Valentine Gallery; Robert C. Vose Galleries, Boston; Weyhe Gallery. *The galleries listed above are in New York unless otherwise noted.*

Preface

Romantic Painting in America is the fifth of a series of books and accompanying exhibitions designed to present the movements, trends or divisions of modern art. The series began in 1936 with *Cubism and Abstract Art*, followed by *Fantastic Art, Dada and Surrealism*, which included a large section devoted to related art of the previous five centuries. In 1938 paintings by modern "primitives" or self-taught artists of Europe, the United States and Canada were exhibited and published under the title *Masters of Popular Painting*. In the spring of 1943 *American Realists and Magic Realists* brought together the pictures of some of the increasing number of living artists who use a comparatively precise, "sharp focus" realism of technique whether their subject matter is actual or imaginary. Their work was introduced by a "preface" of a dozen American paintings chosen from the past one hundred years.

Romantic Painting in America, however, includes the past not as a preface but as an extended "historical" retrospective. "Historical" is here placed in quotation marks because, for the Museum, the history of art ends only with yesterday; the living art of the more remote past is second in interest only to the art of the recent past which we call the present.

This is particularly true of the art of the United States, which, though it is our own, has been less studied and less well understood than European art of the past three hundred years. Not only study and understanding are needed but also active discovery and revaluation—revaluation in the atmosphere of the everchanging climate of contemporary art and critical opinion. With this purpose in mind the Museum has held exhibitions or published books which involved our American past far more than the program and name of the Museum of Modern Art imply. Among these were *Homer, Ryder, Eakins* (1930); *American Folk Art: the Art of the Common Man in America 1750–1900* (1932); *Early Modern Architecture: Chicago 1870–1910* (1933); *George Caleb Bingham, the Missouri Artist* (1935); *Architecture of H. H. Richardson* (1936); *Photography: 1839–1937; Trois siècles d'art aux Etats-Unis* (Paris, 1938); *Indian Art of the United States* (1941); and, already mentioned, *American Realists and Magic Realists* (1943).

It is remarkable that *Romantic Painting in America* should be, so far as we can ascertain, the first general survey of a tradition which now seems to have been at least as strong as the much advertised American love of fact and detailed local color. So vigorous and so manifold is the

Romantic current in American painting that one is easily reconciled to the absence of English, German and French art which would have given international breadth to what the war and our own enthusiasm have confined to national boundaries.

The history of Romanticism in American painting; our little known but important contributions to the beginnings of the European Romantic revolt; what our painters in turn have borrowed from Europe; and, above all, the development of our independent and often individual Romantic art: these are the subjects presented on the following pages by James Thrall Soby. Mr. Soby, the Museum's recently appointed Assistant Director, is not primarily an historian of American art. But he has for years past been a student of early 19th century Romanticism and, more than any other American critic, has heralded the recent revival of Romanticism as distinguished from 20th century realism and abstract art. Dorothy C. Miller, the Museum's Associate Curator of Painting and director of the present exhibition, has chosen the illustrations and edited the biographical notes.

Both Mr. Soby and Miss Miller consider *Romantic Painting in America* something of a pioneer venture, not so much in research, for which time was lacking, but in the general presentation of the subject. They ask that their selections and classifications be considered tentative, particularly insofar as these involve contemporary artists, most of whom are now for the first time brought together in the name of Romanticism. They look forward to the questions and debate which their work may stimulate; even more they hope that the public, both expert and general, will share the excitement and enthusiasm which they and others of the Museum staff have felt in preparing *Romantic Painting in America.*

Alfred H. Barr, Jr.

Romantic Painting in America

What is Romantic painting? And what in particular is American Romantic painting? A vast international documentation deals with the first question. The second has evoked faint reply, though the Romantic literature of such men as James Fenimore Cooper and Edgar Allan Poe has been exhaustively studied here and abroad. To begin then with the first question, Romantic painting represents the temporary triumph of Imagination over Reason in the war between the two which had been openly declared in the 17th century. In historical terms, it commenced to evolve as a formal movement around 1725, reached a climax in the first half of the 19th century and thereafter survived, as it had existed centuries before, as a state of individual mind rather than as a cohesive tendency in art.

The themes of Romantic art were high in emotional content, passionately expounded and regulated only by Instinct—the infallible litmus paper of the Romantics. These themes required to an exceptional degree an intimate communion between artist and audience. And one of the many paradoxes of Romanticism is that its artists, though considering themselves geniuses far removed from the public, should have abetted this communion. They chose subjects which fall into three rough classifications: those to which their audience was emotionally preconditioned, such as scenes from widely read literature; subjects of common firsthand experience—moral causes, dramatic current events, fear, loneliness and pain; and subjects of common nostalgic appeal—the distant in time or place, solitude, sublimity, fantasy. The public to which they appealed was diminished by the very force of their expression, but such as it was, it understood their language.

American Romantic art adopted some of the themes of European Romanticism and much of its spirit. Indeed our Romantic painting came into being in London with Benjamin West, as part of the European movement. It was brought to this country in the early 19th century. The transition was dramatically signalized in 1818 by Washington Allston's decision to return to America to live permanently, after a brilliant career in London. Soon after his arrival Allston wrote: "Another thought recurs, that I had returned to a mighty empire."[1] The statement is significant, for American Romantic painting was at first to feed upon the special grandeur of the American continent, the scale and sweep of its scenery, history and legend. Our 18th century art had been chiefly confined to portraiture and had therefore not developed the intricate Romantic vocabulary of European painting. Consequently our early landscapists took their basic inspiration, direct and raw, from the rich wilderness of nature, first in the East and later in the West. Our figure painters took theirs from the giants of myth and fact and from the lesser heroes of daily life in an untamed country. The native Romantic artist of 1820-50 was less the confessor of egocentric emotion than the celebrant of a national landscape and mythology. Though spiritually akin to his European counterpart, he was on the whole far less introspective.

During the 1840s and 1850s a number of American painters went abroad to study at Düsseldorf, but these were usually realists with only occasional leanings toward Romanticism. Our Romantics went to Paris or London or Rome, and once again the European and American movements drew close together in technique and approach and even in an intense privacy of vision, as with Ryder. But there were important artists who stayed at home and developed a more purely local tradition. Throughout the latter half of the century American Romanticism developed in two divergent but occasionally overlapping directions, native and international. The dual tendency continues to this day. The Francophilia of William Morris Hunt is echoed in the work of many modern American artists; the Romantic regionalism of the Hudson River school has been revived lately in Missouri and Kansas. But that is the end and not the beginning of this brief study. The beginning is with West, Copley and Trumbull.

American Romantic Art Abroad: West, Copley and Trumbull—Proto-Romantics in Figure Painting

In the anti-Rococo reaction which swept over European painting during the latter part of the 18th century, culminating finally in the high Romantic movement, the part played by American artists is gradually coming to be defined. It was an impressive part, and perhaps it could have been played only by men from the New World such as West, Copley and Trumbull. When these painters went to London to live and work, they became identified with the English tradition to such a degree that the more chauvinistic of their countrymen have not yet forgiven them. But they brought to European art certain inextinguishable qualities of mind, formed in their own country and more or less peculiar to it. Among these qualities was a toughness of thought which cherished hard fact both for its own sake and as a starting point in idealization.[2] It is surely no accident that Copley's

[1] Jared B. Flagg, *The Life and Letters of Washington Allston*, New York, 1892, p. 140.

[2] Late in the 19th century William Morris Hunt exclaimed: "'Sentiment' if you like! But do embroider it upon a possibility!" (W. M. Hunt's *Talks on Art*, First Series, Boston, 1875, p. 4.)

single Romantic work, *Watson and the Shark* (ill. p. 49), was inspired by an account of Watson's boyhood rescue from a shark in Havana harbor, a story supposedly heard firsthand by the painter on Copley's first voyage to England in 1774.[3] However Raphaelesque the figure of Watson in Copley's composition, however formalized the crew, the picture carries a new realistic intensity of a kind particular to Romanticism. For the Romantics cherished reality most when its emotional impact was strongest; and grisly, macabre and sensational subjects were so revered that Baudelaire was one day to refer to Romanticism's leading figure in art, Eugène Delacroix, as a "lake of blood." In emotional pitch and journalistic appeal, *Watson and the Shark* foretells by forty-four years the epoch-making *Raft of the Medusa* by the French Romantic, Géricault, and leads to Winslow Homer's *Gulf Stream* (ill. p. 79), painted more than a hundred years later.

An equivalent factual emphasis is to be found in Benjamin West's famous *Death of General Wolfe* (c. 1771) in which, as is well known, West strove for authenticity of detail in the soldiers' uniforms, to the horror of his British contemporaries. Consider that at this same date Jacques Louis David was painting *Combat de Minerve contre Mars Sécouru par Vénus*, supplying Minerva with an upholstered shield and borrowing the figure of Venus from one of Fragonard's pillow fights—consider this, and the revolutionary measure of West's respect for reality may be had. West's precedent was followed by his pupil, John Trumbull, whose *Battle of Bunker's Hill* (1786) was painted from personal experience and whose *Sortie from Gibraltar* (ill. p. 51) is more believable than most battle scenes of the period. Nor was the lesson of West's canvas wasted on David and those of his successors who became the French Romantics. Factual research and direct reportage, especially when related to dramatic subjects heavily involving the emotions, became an important factor in the anti-Rococo approach. In 1793 David was bending over the bloody tub of Marat, sketchbook in hand. Soon after this date Antoine Gros was with Napoleon's armies in Italy as an artist-correspondent. In 1818 Géricault was consulting the survivors of the shipwrecked "Medusa" and building a model of their raft.

Though such dramatic realism lies nearer the main artery of 19th century Romanticism than generally supposed, the pulse of the movement was free imagination, and here again West appears as a precursor. The Romantics laid much stress on choice of subject as a stimulus to flights of the imagination, and in terms of later Romantic development West's iconography is precocious, though less so than that of Fuseli. The Romantics' predilection for the Middle Ages and for the works of Shakespeare is prefigured in his canvases of fifty years before—"as early as 1778 [he was choosing subjects] from early Saxon history; as early as 1789, from Shakespeare . . ."[4] His *Saul and the Witch of Endor* (ill. p. 50) typifies that Romanticism of the supernatural and the wild which,

[3] There is no evidence that Watson traveled from America to England in this year. (Cf. Margaret Jeffery, "A Painting of Copley's English Period," *Bulletin of The Metropolitan Museum of Art*, vol. I, no. 4, December, 1942.)

Fiske Kimball, "Benjamin West in His Historical Significance," *Catalog of the Exhibition of Benjamin West*, Pennsylvania Museum of Art, 1938, p. 11.

springing from the landscapes of Salvator Rosa and his 17th century Italian and Netherlandish contemporaries, was to receive new impetus from the "Gothick" tales of English and German novelists in the late 18th century and was finally to become a recurrent preoccupation among 19th century Romantic artists, particularly but belatedly in France. *Saul and the Witch of Endor* makes an exciting foil to West's previous *Death of General Wolfe.* Between them they illustrate the dual nature of Romanticism's dramatic vocabulary. On the one hand the Romantics often chose subjects of fairly direct emotional force—scenes of death, suffering and injustice. On the other hand they chose subjects which touched man's psychoses—fear of the unknown, the untamed, the darkly metaphysical. At times they struck at the heart of their audience; at others, they probed for its nerves.

Shortly after West's arrival in England he had begun a series of paintings on subjects from heroic antiquity—*Pylades and Orestes, Regulus Returning to Carthage* (which made his fame in England), *The Oath of the Young Hannibal, Hector Taking Leave of Andromache, Erasistratus Discovering the Love of Antiochus and Stratonice.* Such subjects had of course been routine assignments in the European academies since the days of Poussin in Rome; it was the contemporary vitality which West brought to them that constituted his originality. Painted between 1766 and 1774, West's pictures antedate those works of David on equivalent themes which encouraged Frenchmen of the Revolution in their self-identification with the ancient Romans, but it should be kept in mind that David was ten years younger than West. Perhaps it will someday be held that the antiquarianism of West and David formed merely the opening tableau in the Romantic charade—a matter of costume and stage properties rather than an inherently classical manifestation. Whether it is so recognized or not, West has a more direct claim to place as a proto-Romantic in figure painting. His second sketch for *Death on the Pale Horse* (ill. p. 50), completed in 1802 and shown in Paris that year, revives Rubens' Baroque fury of movement, fiery color and turbulent conception, and this at a time when David was still arranging his figures and furniture in an architectonic counterpoint of static and inflexible calm.[5] The sketch for *Death on the Pale Horse* leads directly to the high Romanticism of Delacroix, who looked upon Rubens as the greatest of all artists.[6]

[5] West's picture of 1802 does not, however, quite deserve the solitary, advanced status which has sometimes been claimed for it. In 1801 Antoine Gros had completed the sketch for the *Battle of Nazareth* (Nantes Museum). It is a painting no less indicative of the new Romantic-Baroque spirit than *Death on the Pale Horse,* and probably contributed far more to the cult for Rubens among French Romantics than did West's picture. It is true that West had made a preliminary sketch for his painting before 1796, but this sketch is not comparable to the one under discussion.

[6] Delacroix himself never spoke of Rubens in more enthusiastic terms than did West's pupil, John Trumbull, throughout his visit to France and Germany in 1786. After seeing a famous private collection which included works by Raphael, Titian, Correggio and the Caracci in addition to Rubens, Trumbull wrote: "for color, composition and expression, nothing can excel a Rubens." (*Autobiography, Reminiscences and Letters of John Trumbull from 1756 to 1841,* New York, 1841, p. 113.)

The Migration of Romanticism to America: Washington Allston and Samuel F. B. Morse

West's sketch for *Death on the Pale Horse* is also linked to the work of his pupil, Washington Allston, who was to become the first true, though not consistent, Romantic in American painting. Soon after Allston's arrival in London in 1801, he wrote home: "It is impossible to conceive anything more terrible than Death on the white horse, and I am certain no painter has exceeded Mr. West in the fury, horror, and despair which he has represented in the surrounding figures . . ."[7] In the same letter Allston refers to West as the greatest of contemporary artists in London, but this tribute was probably largely inspired by West's extraordinary personal kindness toward younger painters who enrolled in his studio. Certainly Allston's work showed only sporadic signs of his master's influence and was more directly affected by the paintings of West's English contemporaries. Yet it was fitting that he should have begun his career in West's studio. It had been West's function to launch American art on an international scale. It was to be Allston's to guide native painting to maturity of scope and vision, to broaden the narrow colonial tradition which had limited most of our 18th century artists to portraiture. In so doing he carried over American Romantic painting from one century into the next, from England and the school of Benjamin West to this country and an indigenous art.

Since Allston was born and educated in the 18th century, his career forever reflected that century's ambiguous character as an Age of Reason and as an age of "Gothick" anti-reason. But he lived until 1843 and became a spearhead of 19th century American Romantic painting in both figure and landscape. He had sat with Coleridge as an equal in the Café Greco in Rome and he came home to be a prophet to his countrymen, pointing the way to the Romantic naturalism of the Hudson River school and to the figure painting of the later Romantics. As a key figure in American esthetic development he can scarcely be overestimated.

During his childhood in Waccamaw, South Carolina, Allston absorbed in isolation the melancholy "Gothick" Romanticism which was sweeping over Europe as a formal movement and as a widespread state of mind. He was to express this Romanticism in certain paintings throughout his career, in *The Deluge* (ill. p. 53) and in the *Rise of a Thunderstorm at Sea* (1804), in *Elijah Fed by the Ravens* (1817-18) and in *Spalatro's Vision of the Bloody Hand* (1830-31), inspired by Mrs. Radcliffe's *The Italian.* As a young boy in Carolina he loved the "wild and marvelous."[8] He adds: "I delighted in being terrified by the tales of witches and hags, which the negroes used to tell me . . ."[9] In the Charleston Library he admired engravings for the Boydell Shakespeare Gallery, particularly Fuseli's ghost scene from *Hamlet.* At Harvard as an undergraduate he made drawings

[7] Flagg, *op. cit.*, p. 44.
[8] M. F. Sweetser, *Allston*, Boston, 1879, p. 12.
[9] *Ibid.*, p. 12.

of scenes from *The Mysteries of Udolpho* and Schiller's *The Robbers*; he portrayed a maniac in the act of crushing a dove, and developed the talent for telling ghost stories upon which Washington Irving was later to compliment him. In 1801 when he arrived in England, he was a full-blown Romantic of the 18th century *roman noir* school. "Up to this time," he wrote, "my favorite subjects, with an occasional comic intermission, were banditti. I well remember one of these, where I thought I had happily succeeded in cutting a throat! . . . I did not get rid of this banditti mania until I had been over a year in England."[10]

He did not in fact ever rid himself of this kind of Romantic inspiration, as *Spalatro's Vision of the Bloody Hand*, painted late in life, testifies. But soon after his arrival in London he was caught up in the strong currents of Grand Style tradition which flowed from Italy, and presently he was torn between the fantasist, Fuseli, whom he had admired since youth, and the classicist, Flaxman, whose *Illustrations* he later advised a younger artist to copy every day. He admired equally such Grand Style advocates as Sir Joshua Reynolds and such devotees of exotic invention as John Martin, whose *Sadak in Search of the Waters of Oblivion* (1812) became one of his favorite pictures. The climax to his indecision was reached—inconclusively—in 1804, when he traveled through Paris to spend about four years in Italy, chiefly in Rome. There he looked at the Michelangelo frescoes with no less awe and fervor than the young Géricault was later to experience, but these works did not inspire him to a Romantic figure style of his own as they did Géricault. Instead Allston turned to the 16th century Venetians. He had seen their works in Napoleon's great exhibition in the Louvre (1804) and had written concerning them a letter which may explain why he often abandoned his Romantic approach for a more abstract Mannerism of style. "I . . . *think* I understand *why* so many great colorists, especially Tintoret and Paul Veronese, gave so little heed to the ostensible *stories* of their compositions. In some of them . . . there is not the slightest clue given by which the spectator can guess at the subject. They addressed themselves, not to the senses merely . . . but rather through them to that region (if I may so speak) of the imagination which is supposed to be under the exclusive dominion of music . . ."[11] Thereupon Allston proceeded to earn himself the dubious title "The American Titian," renouncing for long intervals the "Gothick" inspiration so ideally suited to his temperament.

If as a result of this renunciation Allston's Romantic pictures are few in number, they are nonetheless of capital beauty and importance. Most of them are landscapes, and it is in this direction that his main significance appears to lie both for his immediate successors in Romanticism and for posterity. Many of his figure pieces are empty pastiches after 16th century Italian Mannerism or after the Mannerism so variously revived by his English predecessors, Reynolds, Fuseli, Blake, Romney and Lawrence. But his *Deluge* and *Elijah Fed by the Ravens* rank high in terms of historical perspective and for their qualities as painting. His *Rise of a Thunderstorm at Sea* is often appraised as the work which inaugurated the American Romantic landscape school. To it should

[10] *Ibid.*, p. 29. [11] *Ibid.*, pp. 37-38.

be added one of his idyllic landscapes such as the *Diana and Her Nymphs in the Chase* (1805) (ill. p. 52) or the *Italian Landscape* (1827) which revived the tradition of elegiac pastorals several years before Corot's first efforts in this direction. These pictures and the magnificent *Moonlit Landscape* (c. 1827) (ill. p. 52) reveal the reverse side of Allston's Romantic naturalism—a vision of calm loveliness as opposed to the rugged torment of his *roman noir* settings. The open, abstract patterns of cloud and sky in the *Moonlit Landscape* foretell Ryder's handling of similar passages with startling exactitude. The idyllic spirit of its composition was adopted by a number of later landscapists, among them Inness and Wyant.

To Allston's house in Cambridgeport, Massachusetts, came a long procession of the celebrated men of his period, and his limited production as a painter during the last twenty-five years of his life was ascribed by Dunlap to his love of conversation. The charge was indignantly denied by Allston, and there is in fact a more plausible reason why his output slackened. The reason lies in his huge unfinished composition, *Belshazzar's Feast*, the story of which is a far greater Romantic fantasy, in the contemporary, Surrealist sense of the term, than anything Allston ever painted or said. The picture, measuring roughly 12 by 16 feet, was nearly completed when Allston left London in 1818. When he died a great part of the composition had been painted out, so that for twenty-five years he had more or less steadily worked backwards to the raw canvas.[12] There are a number of conflicting theories as to why this should have happened: it was said that Gilbert Stuart persuaded him to change the perspective, resulting in "more than twenty thousand chalk-lines in circles and arcs, to bring the amended figures into correct drawing"[13]; that financial worries spoiled his ability to concentrate; that John Martin's picture on the same subject, shown in London in 1821, dulled his own ambition. The true explanation probably springs from inner rather than external circumstance, for Allston's interminable references to the picture in letters of the period make clear that he had developed a thoroughly paranoiac attitude toward it. He defended it bitterly against real and imagined abuse, he guarded it so zealously that on one occasion he demanded that workmen going to his studio should enter with their backs to it. He felt that he could not die before he finished it, and when he did die, leaving a half-wrecked canvas, his close friend, R. H. Dana, Jr., wrote thankfully in his diary: "He had escaped that terrible vision—the nightmare, the incubus, the tormentor of his life—his unfinished picture."[14]

The story of *Belshazzar's Feast* is Balzac's *Chef d'Oeuvre Inconnu* come to life and no inconsiderable part of Romantic history. Fortunately Allston as a person accounted for more positive contributions, and among these is his share in forming the career of his devoted pupil, Samuel

[12] The fact is the more surprising in that Allston ordinarily worked with a quick, instinctive ease. His *Elijah Fed by the Ravens* was finished in three weeks, and he once wrote a young artist: "Do not be anxious, but put faith in your fingers. When I paint, I often do not look at my palette; I take off my colors by a secret sympathy between my hand and the pigments." (Sweetser, *op. cit.*, p. 141.)

[13] *Ibid.*, p. 121.

[14] Flagg, *op. cit.*, p. 333.

F. B. Morse. Though Morse went to London, exhibited in the Royal Academy and received the usual encouragement from West, he worshipped Allston and in 1813 wrote home: "You must recollect, when you tell friends that I am studying in England, that I am a pupil of Mr. Allston, and not Mr. West."[15]

Since Morse became primarily a portrait painter between the time of his return from Europe in 1815 and his absorption in telegraphy, Romanticism's influence on his work is minor and sporadic. Yet in 1828 he responded to the appeal of the Greek War of Independence, an obsessive theme for Delacroix and endless lesser Romantics and the equivalent of the recent Spanish Civil War in our own century as a moral cause. In that year Morse painted *The Greek Boy* (cat. no. 151), its subject a youthful survivor of the Massacre of Chios who had been ransomed from the Turks by a group of Americans and sent to this country for adoption. The boy, Christos Evangelides, arrived in New York in 1828 and was a great attraction in literary and artistic circles. Morse painted his portrait in full Oriental costume, with Greek and Turk warriors struggling in the background, and William Cullen Bryant composed a poem, *The Greek Boy*, in his honor. Portrait and poem are part of the ample body of evidence to prove that one of Romanticism's deepest nostalgias was directed toward antiquity, even toward its modern vestiges. In 1832 Delacroix, after traveling all the way to Morocco in search of contemporary exoticism, was elated to discover that the Moroccans reminded him of the ancient Greeks and Romans. Toward the end of the century John La Farge reacted similarly to the Samoans he saw in the South Seas.[16]

Morse's *Chapel of the Virgin at Subiaco* (1830) (ill. p. 56), is closely related in conception to the Italian landscapes of such German Romantics as Franz Catel, Carl Gustav Carus and Philipp Fohr. But Morse reserved his longest flight of imagination for a native subject—New York University at Washington Square. His *Allegorical Landscape Showing New York University* is an astonishing transmutation of fact to fancy, a vision of lakeside landscape and imaginative architecture which must have confounded both students and faculty of the University. It would be interesting to know whether the picture influenced Cole's landscapes with architecture, such as *The Departure* and *The Return* (1837) and *The Architect's Dream* (1840). In any case Morse might have himself developed into a painter of considerable Romantic interest had he not devoted himself to the invention and perfecting of the telegraph. The invention was to be anti-Romantic for American artists later than Morse. Half a century afterwards, in explaining why he was going to the South Seas, John La Farge wrote: "We wished to go very far. Japan is too near. There is always the telegraph. The Pacific gives you at least two months free from news."[17]

[15] Sweetser, *op. cit.*, p. 64.

[16] In describing the Samoans, La Farge wrote that they had startled him "with a great wonder that no one had told me of a rustic Greece still alive somewhere, and still to be looked at." (John La Farge, *Reminiscences of the South Seas*, New York, 1912, p. 86.)

[17] J. Walker McSpadden, *Famous Painters of America*, New York, 1907, p. 220.

The Triumph of Nature:
The Hudson River School and The Glorification of The West

For many European Romantics of the early 19th century America was a rugged Arcadia to the West—for Shelley afire with justice no less than for Coleridge conjuring up an escapist image of life on the Susquehanna. American Romantics of the period shared this conception of their country, and their works became to a large extent an art of moral sentiments and landscape. As such it developed certain close affinities to Romantic painting in England and, above all, in Germany. It stood in opposition to French Romantic art, in which figure painting remained so supreme that Delacroix spoke with contempt of landscape painters, while Baudelaire declared that landscape appealed to lazy, sluggish and unimaginative artists. The Americans were capable of replying in kind. When Thomas Cole visited the exhibition of contemporary French art in the Louvre in 1831, he wrote: "Although I had been informed that the present French artists were low in merit, I did not expect to find them, with little exception, so totally devoid of it. I was disgusted in the beginning with their subjects. Battle, murder and death, Venuses and Psyches, the bloody and the voluptuous, are the things in which they seem to delight . . ."[18] Later on, in writing to the art historian, Dunlap, Cole passionately defended landscape painting, asserting that it was more difficult than historical and superior in everything save passion.[19]

For the generation of painters which afterwards came to be known as the Hudson River, Catskills or White Mountains school, not only was landscape a greater form of art than figure painting but American landscape was more inspiring than European. Behind this judgment was the authority of Jean Jacques Rousseau's philosophy of primitivism, reexpressed by Cole and William Cullen Bryant, the two leading American prophets of nature Romanticism. "All nature here is new to art," Cole wrote, "No Tivolis, Ternis, Mont Blancs, Plinlimmons, hackneyed and worn by the daily pencils of hundreds; but primeval forests, virgin lakes and waterfalls . . ."[20] And Bryant, delivering his famous funeral oration for Cole, said: "I well remember . . . the delight which was expressed at the opportunity of contemplating pictures which carried the eye over scenes of wild grandeur peculiar to our country, over our aerial mountaintops with their mighty growth of forest never touched by the axe, along the banks of streams never deformed by culture, and into the depth of skies bright with the hues of our own climate . ."[21] The two men and their whole philosophy of Romanticism are summarized in Asher Durand's portrait, *Kindred Spirits* (ill. p. 57).

[18] Louis L. Noble, *The Course of Empire, Voyage of Life, and Other Pictures of Thomas Cole, N.A.*, New York, 1853, pp. 125-26.
[19] *Ibid.*, pp. 171-72.
[20] *Ibid.*, p. 202.
[21] *Ibid.*, pp. 58-59.

It is generally believed that Cole's earliest landscapes were preceded a few years by those of Thomas Doughty. But except in rare cases such as *In Nature's Wonderland* (cat. no. 79) with its elaborately curvilinear composition, Doughty's art was a simple, straightforward transcription of nature as it appeared to a man of limited imagination and skillful hands. Cole, on the contrary, brought to landscape decided imaginative power, evident not only in the landscapes themselves but in the architectural fantasies with which he often filled them. He also brought to his art a passionate moral force which made him the acknowledged leader and prophet of nature Romanticism in this country. In contrast to the French landscapists, whose veneration for nature was rooted in a peasant humility, to the Englishman, William Blake, who declared that "Nature is the devil," Cole made his art a sermon on the godlike relation of nature to man, as many of the German Romantics had done. He did so with a vigor of conception which transcends the sentimental piety of his period and sometimes comes through with clarity and force, as in *The Expulsion from Eden* (ill. p. 54).[22] He prayed before he painted, and often his sermons required prolonged attendance by his audience, as in his four epic series, *The Departure* and *The Return*, *Before* and *After*, *The Course of Empire* and the *Voyage of Life*.

Cole was born in England and lived there until he was nineteen. Returning for a visit in 1829, he found his own works superior to those of the contemporary English, though he admired Turner, Wilson and Calcott. Ten years later he traveled on the Continent and praised the paintings of Titian, Correggio, Claude, Poussin and (prophecy of the Pre-Raphaelite Brotherhood) painters earlier than Raphael. He declared that Italy was a paradise for painters, but added characteristically: "I have found, though, no natural scenery yet which has affected me so powerfully as that which I have seen in the wilderness places of America: and although there are a peculiar softness and beauty in Italian skies, ours are far more gorgeous."[23]

Despite this patriotic statement, Cole's art was based upon the 17th century European tradition to a degree from which no love of New World scenery could completely free him. As opposed to Asher B. Durand and other contemporaries who often narrowed their view of nature to a detailed close-up, Cole was a painter of vistas, modeling his compositions on Claude. "I am not a mere leaf-painter," he protested. "I have higher conceptions than a mere combination of inanimate, uninformed nature."[24] Nevertheless, it is the detail in Cole's works which is often so specifically American in its unchecked tangle of trees, rocks and underbrush, though to examine it is to go directly counter to Cole's own wish. He declared that detail should not attract the eye, and

[22] This painting seems to abound in the currently fashionable "double images"—forms which suggest other forms of a different identity. There is some evidence that their presence may have been deliberate. "Treading the mosses of the forest," Cole wrote, "my attention has often been attracted by the appearance of action and expression of surrounding objects, especially of trees. I have been led to reflect upon the fine effects they produce, and to look into the causes. They spring from some resemblance to the human form." (Noble, *op. cit.*, p. 65.)

[23] *Ibid.*, p. 142.

[24] *Ibid.*, p. 263.

to make sure that it did not do so, he painted his skies first on the canvas, keying them up to such a point that they tended to silhouette the foreground. Perhaps to Cole's example may be partially ascribed the emphasis on backlighting so common in 19th century American painting. His predilection for objects "seen between the spectator and the sun"[25] was inherited by numerous native painters of later generations.

Cole died in 1848, revered by American artists and writers, a national figure through the fame of his *Voyage of Life* series. Toward the end of his life he lamented that he had not lived in a time and place where a more cultivated taste prevailed, believing that had he done so he would have conceived more sublime works. He does not appear to have doubted his ability to execute them, though his technical limitations were serious and have accounted for his eclipse. After Cole the Romantic tradition moved more or less steadily away from philosophy toward esthetics, from ideology toward craftsmanship. The progress is marked in midcourse by the landscapes of Kensett and Whittredge, so superior in painterly quality to Cole's works, and reaches its climax in the "art for art's sake" doctrine adopted by Hunt, La Farge and Whistler.

A significant factor in this development is the fact that a number of Cole's successors studied or made a profession of engraving, a trade which focused attention on technical problems and reduced conception to an imitative role. Chief among these men was Cole's contemporary, Asher Brown Durand, whose first landscape, according to his son's biography, was exhibited in the National Academy of Design in 1828. From 1832 on, Durand painted landscapes consistently, alternating them with genre and historical compositions (he abandoned the last-named category in the late 1830s). Around 1834 Durand wrote Cole: "I am still willing to confess myself a trespasser on your ground, though, I trust, not a poacher; landscape still occupies my attention."[26] The quotation serves to confirm Cole's position as leader of the landscape school, yet Durand was justified in saying that he was not a poacher. His fundamental approach to landscape was radically different from Cole's, as different as Courbet's from that of Corot. Durand's long career as an engraver taught him a respect for the very detail which Cole had held in careful check, and in his work the influence of the 17th century, formalist landscape tradition is less often felt. Indeed, in the winter of 1840-41 he wrote Cole a far from enthusiastic letter giving his reactions to the landscapes of Claude. By contrast with Cole's epic attitude toward nature, Durand regarded landscape as a series of conjoined but separable still lifes, and late in life he advised a younger artist: "You will be most successful in the more simple and solid materials, such as rocks and tree-trunks, and, after these, earth-banks and the coarser kinds of grass . . ."[27]

Whereas Cole lived in intimate communion with nature and retired to his studio to compose its elements from sketches, Durand resided in New York City for fifty-one years of his life and

[25] *Ibid.*, p. 262.
[26] John Durand, *The Life and Times of A. B. Durand*, New York, 1894, p. 140.
[27] *Ibid.*, p. 215.

made excursions to the country to paint directly from nature. As a result Durand tended to bring nature Romanticism down to earth, to reduce its ideological content from the sermon to the anecdote, its pictorial form from the vista to the section. His favorite poets were Goldsmith and Thomson (Cole's were Dante, Milton and Wordsworth), and there is in most of his work a simple, pastoral realism which relates him to Doughty rather than to Cole. Yet he was not entirely immune to the more intellectual Romantic forces of his period, as may be seen in *Kindred Spirits* (1849) (ill. p. 57), *Thanatopsis* (1850) and *Primeval Forest* (c. 1869-70).

As a youth John F. Kensett, whom James Jackson Jarves was to call "the Bryant of our painters,—a little sad and monotonous, but sweet, artistic, and unaffected,"[28] applied to Durand to be taken as an apprentice in engraving. He was refused, since Durand, twenty-two years Kensett's senior, was by then ready to abandon engraving. The young artist thereupon studied the process with his own uncle, and the evidence of this training is often visible in his work, reinforced by his schooling in Düsseldorf. A number of his paintings are in the Durand tradition of minute exactitude in rendering close-ups of nature, though they are usually more polished in technique. But Kensett was born with a sensitivity to mood and hour which his hearty predecessor lacked, and much of his art is a direct negation of Durand's premise that nature is the ultimate truth, a premise expressed by Durand in a statement which might have been written by the Realist, Courbet: "There is not . . . any charm that the most inventive imagination ever employed . . . that is not to be seen in Nature, more beautiful and more fitting than art has ever realized or ever can."[29] Unlike Durand, Kensett worked from sketches rather than from nature direct. Though few of his landscapes are as arbitrarily fabricated as Cole's, in the best of his works (ill. p. 68) he manipulated the atmosphere with a subtlety of taste and effect which forecasts the work of George Inness, Homer D. Martin and William Morris Hunt. He relied, sometimes with astonishingly beautiful results, on an infiltration of poetic feeling in interpreting the light and air of his subjects. To the simplest themes he brought a new delicacy of emotion, a soft-spoken poesy of nuance which gives him a particular if minor place in American 19th century landscape art. Probably as a result of his seven years in Europe, the frontier spirit is conspicuously absent in many of his works. (Symbolically he often painted the curved and open coastline, looking to the sea and Europe.) For him nature was not always God, as it was for Cole, nor Truth, as it was for Durand. It was the rhyme of the sonnet and the trill of the flute, to be read and heard in a rare and dwindling hour.

In one of Durand's letters to a younger artist he wrote: "All the license that the artist can claim or desire is to choose the time and place where Nature displays her chief perfections, whether of beauty or majesty, repose or action."[30] The dictum was accepted at face value by many land-

[28] James Jackson Jarves, *The Art-Idea*, New York (fourth edition), 1877, p. 235.

[29] From Durand's letters to a young artist. Quoted from G. W. Sheldon, *American Painters*, New York (enlarged edition), 1881, p. 132.

[30] G. W. Sheldon, *op. cit.*, p. 132.

scape painters of the generation which succeeded his own, and the work of men like Jasper Francis Cropsey constitutes an index to those regions of America and Europe within which selection of landscape subjects might safely be made. For Durand the fields of Hoboken had sufficed for a time, for Cropsey the landscape of England, for Worthington Whittredge the countryside surrounding Düsseldorf. But there were artists of this generation who believed nature's "chief perfections" were farther to seek and who joined the long line of 19th century artists traveling far in search of the unspoiled and the exotic. Frederick Edwin Church, a pupil of Cole, belongs to this group. In 1853 and again in 1857 he went to South America and came home with numerous sketches which resulted in such pictures as *Cotopaxi, Ecuador* (ill. p. 66). The choice of subject in this picture is meaningful. Since the mid-18th century the Romantic cult for mountains had been steadily growing in intensity. By 1826, the year of Church's birth, few European mountain ranges remained unexplored in fact or fancy; the Romantics were finally running out of mountains. Church, finding the Catskills inadequate, solved the dilemma by going to Ecuador to sketch Cotopaxi, rising nearly 19,000 feet in the Andes. The mountain was not only high but volcanic, a fact of particular interest to the Romantics, for whom much of nature's fascination lay in its constant menace to mankind. Moreover, Church's choice of subject emphasizes the process of exteriorization which Romantic inspiration was undergoing. Whereas Baudelaire had referred to Delacroix as a "volcano artistically concealed by a bouquet of flowers," now the volcano became a natural wonder to be visited by man. In the one case Romanticism consisted in an inner tumult of imagination; in the other it required strong legs for travel.

Having explored the tropics of South America, Church soon determined to see and paint their absolute antithesis in Romantic iconography—the icefields of the North to which Mary Shelley's Frankenstein monster had lumbered in search of peace. Church's interest in the subject had perhaps been stimulated by Durand's engraving of an iceberg which the latter had seen and sketched on his return trip from Europe in 1841.[31] In any case Church read contemporary accounts of the northern wastelands and finally sailed for Labrador, returning with sketches from which he painted several pictures of icebergs. The subject had tremendous Romantic appeal in that it combined an exoticism of the unfamiliar with a Rousseauvian exoticism of the uninhabited.[32]

Both kinds of exoticism were to be found in Church's own country and were there discovered, twenty-five years after George Catlin had opened the American West to artists, by the German-born landscapist, Albert Bierstadt. In 1858 Bierstadt joined General Lander's expedition and worked northwest from St. Louis to the Nebraska Territory and southern Oregon. His presence

[31] The theme had also been treated by the German Romantic, Caspar David Friedrich, a fact which serves to emphasize the spiritual kinship between American and German Romantic painters during the first half of the 19th century.

[32] Since Audubon's journals were not published until later in the century, few had read his disenchanting comment of June 23, 1833, on his own trip to Labrador. In complaining of the Fur Company's inroads, he wrote: "Where can I go now, and visit nature undisturbed?" (Donald Culross Peattie, ed., *Audubon's America*, Boston, 1940, p. 238.)

in the expedition is an indication of a rising scientism within the Romantic movement, implicit in Bierstadt's paintings of the Rockies (ill. p. 67) and prefigured in the documentary art of Catlin and Audubon (ill. pp. 60 and 59). Certain artists now came to feel that their work should have an added justification as scientific documentation; the spirit persisted until the overwhelming estheticism of the late 19th century made science the subservient handmaiden of art itself. Not only art lovers but cartographers, botanists and geologists admired Bierstadt's pictures, and much of his interest for his contemporaries lay in the supposed accuracy with which he represented the unfamiliar.

Many of Bierstadt's paintings depict buffaloes—an animal introduced by Catlin to the vast menagerie founded by the high Romantic movement and even now being added to by such modern artists as Darrel Austin and Morris Graves (ill. pp. 128 and 126). The cult for animals had begun in England, where private zoos were a requisite of the Romantic's estate. From England the cult had spread to France, but in that country the more economical Romantic hero had been content to have the State support his animals and had gone to visit them at the Jardin des Plantes. By the early 19th century public zoos were sufficiently naturalistic in planning so that visitors such as Géricault, Delacroix and Barye could convince themselves that they were face to face with lions and tigers in their native habitat. But this was a different matter from Catlin's and Bierstadt's experiences in the American West. There animals were both fierce and free, and on one occasion a companion of Bierstadt wounded a buffalo slightly to permit the painter to stand near and sketch its death charge. Another companion was within reason in writing of this event: "I doubt if there be any other country but Kansas and Nebraska where the brush follows so hard on the rifle . . ."[33]

Bierstadt's interest in the awesome scenery of the American West is echoed a generation later in such a painting as Thomas Moran's *Cliffs of the Upper Colorado River, Wyoming Territory* of 1882 (ill. p. 76). Meanwhile, in the East, a quieter and more lyric Romantic landscape was being evolved, an art founded on a sensitive interpretation of nature's less declamatory moods. *Blue Hole, Flood Waters, Little Miami River* (ill. p. 65) by the Negro, Robert S. Duncanson, exemplifies the new tendency, but a more striking example is afforded by *Storm Approaching Larchmont Bay* (ill. p. 70), painted in 1868 by the little-known artist, M. J. Heade. In Heade's composition the towering verticals of Bierstadt's mountain scenery have disappeared, to be replaced by a horizontal disposition of forms which is in itself symptomatic of a new repose in the Romantic spirit. The thunderous opera of the 1830 generation was nearing its end, its players and audience alike exhausted by its passion of gesture and rhetoric. The time was ripe for a more professional landscape art in which dramaturgy would count less than sensitivity and finish. Heade's lovely *Larchmont Bay*, though reactionary in technique, leads to the new nature Romanticism of George Inness' late career. Meanwhile American figure painting was undergoing a separate development from the 1820s to the Civil War.

[33] Henry T. Tuckerman, *American Artist Life*, New York, 1867, p. 392.

Romantic Figure Painting of Americana; New York to the West

In the late 1820s, when Cole was beginning to found the Romantic landscape tradition in this country, a native Romantic figure painting was being developed by John Quidor, born in 1801 near the Washington Irving country and a resident of New York City nearly all his life. There was, however, the important difference that, while Cole was accepted as a prophet and master, Quidor was almost unknown to his contemporaries and exerted little or no influence over the art of his period. His earliest known painting, dated 1823, was of a scene from *Don Quixote*, and he subsequently took a majority of his subjects from literature, particularly from that of his countrymen, Washington Irving and James Fenimore Cooper.

Quidor's *Ichabod Crane Pursued by the Headless Horseman of Sleepy Hollow* was exhibited in 1828 and inaugurated a career devoted to horror Romanticism—a depiction of witchery, dark legend and terror—which if anything intensified the macabre humor of its literary sources. There are broad traces of European influence in Quidor's work, but none is so specific as might appear at first glance. His figures seem a strange compound of Bosch and Magnasco. The pop-eyed caricatural handling of the heads instantly calls Daumier to mind, yet this treatment occurs in Quidor's earliest paintings, at a time when he could hardly have known the work of the French master, who was his junior by seven years. Nor does it seem likely that he knew the works of his slightly younger German contemporary, Moritz von Schwind, often so closely related to his own. A more likely source of Quidor's figures is in the drawings of Hogarth and Rowlandson, whose crusty vigor he shares. But Quidor's contours are notable for a mannered elegance quite different from that of the Englishmen, and at times almost suggest a deliberate parody on the Italian Mannerist and Baroque figure styles. Lacking more definite evidence, we must assume that Quidor was a "natural" Romantic whose art evolved from the recesses of a distraught and powerful imagination.

His landscapes are in the tradition of the 17th century *banditti* school but parallel the action of the figures to an extent that Quidor's predecessors would have considered beyond credulity's province. In many of his canvases nature is more than a sympathetic backdrop to outlaw activity, as it was so often in the 17th century; it is a conniving and active agent in this activity. The background trees and rocks of *Leatherstocking Meets the Law* of 1832 (cat. no. 174) parallel exactly the compositional action of the figures. In *The Money Diggers* (ill. p. 58) the foreground figure and tree are nearly identical in pose and intent, while the remainder of the landscape writhes with its own sinister activity. For Quidor man and nature were related in evil far more intimately than Cole had attempted to relate them for good.

At almost exactly the time when Quidor was painting his earliest important pictures, the first prints of John James Audubon's great folio, *The Birds of America*, were being mailed to subscribers. Thus to the art of the Eastern Romantic there was opposed the art of an ornithologist whose material had been collected in wide peregrinations through the South and Midwest. The work of Quidor was, of course, more truly and recognizably Romantic than that of Audubon. Yet if Quidor was the illustrator of an openly Romantic literature, Audubon was the illustrator of a science which was not without its Romantic overtones. The quest of birds was in a limited sense a quest of the unknown and the exotic. However dispassionately it may have been conducted, it was an exploration of the trees and underbrush—nature's tenements—with their darting, colorful life of migration, nesting and song. And Audubon's prints, as is well known, were totally different from the prints of earlier ornithologists. While striving for realism of detail and habitat Audubon succeeded, perhaps unconsciously, in dramatizing his subjects beyond the requirements of ornithological research. Certain of his prints, such as the *White-headed Eagle* (cat. no. 7), reflect the savage grandeur of the struggle for survival as powerfully as Delacroix's studies of stallions fighting on the sands of Algiers. Audubon's *Quadrupeds of America*, begun in 1845, contains plates like that of the *Canada Lynx* (ill. p. 59) in which the psychology of the animal is stressed as much as its coloration and habitat. In his basic attitude toward animals Audubon was part and parcel of his time—the high period of the Romantic movement.[34] He studied birds and quadrupeds objectively but appreciated and interpreted their instinctive savage wisdom, which so many Romantics considered superior to man's untidy and vacillating logic. At times and in certain subjects he was as much of a Romantic *animalier* as the French sculptor, Antoine Louis Barye.

As later, in the case of Winslow Homer, the Romantic cast to some of Audubon's work has been obscured by the artist's avowed contempt for the workings of free imagination. Though Audubon was born in Santo Domingo of a French father, his early manhood in this then Puritan country apparently taught him to be embarrassed by emotional extravagance. His own writing is primarily factual, and he disparaged the Romantic tendencies in the prose of the younger scientist-painter, George Catlin. Catlin had traveled through the American Indian country for eight years, beginning in 1832, with the fixed purpose of making an extensive graphic document of the Indian's disappearing culture (ill. p. 60). In 1843 Audubon followed his footsteps to the Yellowstone country to collect material for his own *Quadrupeds of America*. On May 17 he noted in his journal: "Ah! Mr. Catlin, I am now sorry to see and to read your accounts of the Indians *you* saw—how very different they must have been from any that I have seen! We saw here no 'carpeted prairies,' no 'velvety distant landscape'; and if these things are to be seen, why, the sooner we reach them the better."[35] On June 11 he added: "We have seen much remarkably handsome scenery, but nothing at all comparing with Catlin's descriptions; his book must, after all, be altogether a humbug."[36]

[34] To appreciate the change in attitude toward animals which came in with the Romantic movement, one has only to compare one of Delacroix's lions to the famous painting of a hippopotamus by the 18th century artist, Pietro Longhi. In Longhi's picture, the hippopotamus is a circus animal, led docilely past a balcony of festival figures. In Delacroix's works the lion is free, menacing and restored to its natural identity as king of the beasts.

[35] Peattie, *op. cit.*, p. 282.

[36] *Ibid.*, p. 298.

Catlin's book was far from a humbug, but it was certainly Romantic and it remains an impressive refutation of the theory that love of science thrives best in frigid hearts. No sooner had Catlin arrived at the upper Missouri, at the beginning of his travels, than he was comparing the Indians to the models of ancient Greek sculpture.[37] The Missouri River was described in a passage which Mrs. Radcliffe could scarcely have improved: "There is a redeeming beauty in the green and carpeted shores, which hem in this huge and terrible deformity of waters . . . where the mighty forests of stately cottonwood stand, and frown in horrid dark and coolness over the filthy abyss below . . ."[38] And later on, warming to his subject, he wrote of the same scenery: "A place where the mind could think volumes; but the tongue must be silent that would *speak*, and the hand palsied that would *write*. A place where a Divine would confess that he had never fancied Paradise—where the painter's palette would lose its beautiful tints—the blood-stirring notes of eloquence would die in their utterance—and even the soft tones of sweet music would scarcely preserve a spark to light the soul again that had passed this sweet delirium."[39] He concluded with the words, "I mean the prairie . . .", and so he did.

It is not known whether Catlin's rhapsodic accounts of the Missouri country were read by Missouri's own George Caleb Bingham. In any case they can have had little effect, for while Catlin came to the frontier as a Romantic scientist from the East, Bingham lived in Missouri from early youth and knew its history, legend and daily incident from long and continuous experience. To Catlin the territory had appealed as a virgin land inhabited by redskinned Greeks; to Bingham it was the new America, explored and founded by men of extraordinary vigor and cunning. But Bingham's paintings, for all their closer bond with reality, are no less Romantic than Catlin's and have acquired enormous nostalgic interest over the hundred years since they were painted.

The story that Bingham was dramatically introduced to painting by watching Chester Harding paint a portrait of Daniel Boone has lately come under suspicion.[40] Whether it is true or not, Bingham's mature style—the style of his best genre pictures of the '40s and '50s, as opposed to his early portraits and his late works, painted on his return from Düsseldorf—was almost certainly inspired by his trip to Philadelphia in 1837. He studied in the Academy of Fine Arts for three months and saw the genre paintings of Henry Inman and John Neagle's genre portrait of the blacksmith, Pat Lyons. It seems likely that the latter picture impressed him deeply and accounted in good part for his conversion from a straight portrait painter to a genre artist dealing with

[37] When Benjamin West was shown the Apollo in Rome, he had remarked: "How like a young Mohawk warrior!" [William Dunlap, *A History of the Rise and Progress of the Arts of Design in the United States*, (new edition), Boston, 1918, vol. I, p. 48.]

Apparently the comparison could work both ways. When Catlin arrived in Paris in 1845 with his troupe of Indians, Delacroix found their nobility of mien and gesture equivalent to that of antique sculpture. (Cf. Raymond Escholier, *Delacroix*, Paris, 1927, vol. II, p. 302.)

[38] George Catlin, *Illustrations of the Manners, Customs and Condition of the North American Indians: in a Series of Letters and Notes*. London, 1845 (fifth edition), vol. I, p. 18.

[39] *Ibid.*, vol. II, p. 3.

[40] Cf. Albert Christ-Janer, *George Caleb Bingham of Missouri*, New York, 1940, p. 13.

recognizable personalities. Returning to Missouri, he designed a banner for the Whig Convention of 1840 at Rocheport which bore the superb slogan, "Old Tippecanoe and Tyler too." He made a number of drawings of scenes of local stump oratory, involving numerous figures, and he was soon launched as a genre painter.

Bingham's *Fur Traders Descending the Missouri* (ill. p. 61) is one of his earliest genre works, and perhaps the most Romantic painting of his known career—a haunting and haunted masterpiece. In its almost Oriental economy, its wonderful atmospheric effect, its soft gradation of space, its sensitivity to the light, air and glassy motion of the river—in all these, it is an unforgettable work of art. The ghostly pirogue slides into view from nowhere; its figures stare straight at their audience, and in the prow sits the Poe-like bear, object of civilization's wonder and curiosity and symbol of the fur traders' hard, free life in the great woods.

The hardier side of Bingham's Romantic nature is reflected in *Daniel Boone Escorting a Band of Pioneers into the Western Country* (ill. p. 61), showing Boone (without the coonskin cap which he is said to have loathed), his wife, daughter and companions coming over the mountains like ancient prophets, in full consciousness of the epic moment which was theirs. The emotional impact of the scene is acute; perhaps no other episode in American frontier history had been so grandly presented in a painting. The grouping of the figures is masterly, as it nearly always was with Bingham, attesting his knowledge of engravings from the Renaissance and Baroque and explained in part by his practice of working up his compositions from numerous sketches. The landscape seems based on those of the Hudson River painters or their 17th century models. But Bingham's landscape is more real and powerful. Storms have passed through it with a more abrupt and wilder vengeance: every tree and log in the foreground has been splintered; their wounds are portrayed as such rather than as pastoral properties of the Romantic vista. The picture is an invaluable addition to Romantic Americana. Taken with the *Fur Traders* and the other works of Bingham's mid-career, it seems to justify the artist in "whispering sometimes to myself, that in the familiar line which I have chosen, I am the greatest among all the disciples of the brush, which my native land has yet produced."[41]

In the documentary and figure painting of Audubon, Catlin and Bingham, as in the landscapes of Bierstadt, Moran and Thomas Hill, the American West came into its own as a wellspring of pictorial Romantic inspiration, rivaled only by the Old South. The West's fullest exploitation awaited the invention of the moving pictures, but meanwhile its Romantic hold was steadily increased through art, literature and song. The almost forgotten artist, Alfred J. Miller (1810-74), traveled through the Rocky Mountains in 1837, only five years after Catlin's excursion, and painted a number of pictures of Indian life, most of which are now in Scotland. The finest of them, such as the *Buffalo Hunt* (ill. p. 60), deserve greater recognition than they have received. This recognition has been given instead to two artists of a later generation (both were

[41] From a letter by Bingham written in Philadelphia in 1853 (Christ-Janer, *op. cit.*, p. 77).

born in the 1860s), Frederic Remington and Charles M. Russell, who popularized the West's two principal and opposing dramatic figures—the Indian and the cowboy. Both men were ideally equipped for their function. Their art was easily understood; it was skillful illustration; it was accepted as true by the cowboys and by Theodore Roosevelt; it was expensive but widely reproduced. In short, it was suited to become a natural target for a later generation's scorn. Yet it is honest popular art and occasionally combines a rather impressive technical virtuosity with a certain direct emotional appeal, as in the illustration on page 76. Nevertheless, the Far West still awaits an interpreter of real authority in art. Though a number of the most talented modern artists live and work there—C. S. Price, Darrel Austin, Morris Graves, Matthew Barnes—none of them primarily records the local scene. The Far West has had no Bingham as Missouri had; it has badly needed a Winslow Homer or even an Eastman Johnson. Such an interpreter may even now appear, since of all Romantic lands the American West has shown the strongest immunity to disenchantment.

Romantic Painting After 1850

1. Page and Inness

At some point shortly after the mid-century—difficult to make precise but broadly signalized by this nation's greatest emotional experience, the Civil War—the pioneer era of American Romantic painting came to an end. Our artists continued to draw inspiration from the local scene, in both landscape and figure painting, but they no longer received so strong a metaphysical impetus from the newness, wildness and size of their country as had the earlier Romantics.[42] Their conception of America was particular rather than abstract, and they described it in terms of a more private response than their predecessors, in a language freer of New World dialect. They tended to center their careers not so much upon the wonder of citizenship in a new and powerful nation as upon international intellectual faiths, esthetic, religious or both. Among them were the two Swedenborgians, William Page and George Inness.

Page was born in Albany in 1811, and studied under Samuel Morse in his extreme youth. He prepared for the ministry at Andover Theological Seminary and Amherst but then decided to become a portrait painter. In 1849 he sailed for Rome, remained for eleven years and there acquired that curious eclecticism of style which is so apparent in his *Portrait of Mrs. Page* (ill. p. 69). The picture suggests a Pre-Raphaelite Ingres in low key, yet its peculiar intensity of expression is Page's own and recalls his dictum: "A true likeness shows one inside out."[43] The author of *New Geometrical Method of Measuring the Human Figure*, Page developed a Romantic theory of portraiture which combined a faith in geometric laws of proportion with phrenology. In contrast to

[42] Even Winslow Homer's sea paintings, which seem an immediate refutation of this statement, were first inspired by the seacoast of Tynemouth, England.
[43] Sheldon, *op. cit.*, p. 222.

the usual 19th century portraitists, whose attitude toward their subjects was matter-of-fact and realistic, he had a supernatural, cosmic conception of his chosen field and was perhaps the purest American Romantic in it. "The order of Nature," he wrote, "is fixed in portraits as in planets."[44]

Page worshipped Titian's paintings and spent much of his time attempting to discover the secret of the Venetian's technique. He constantly experimented on his own with the materials of art, so that a number of his paintings have destroyed themselves through chemical reaction. His efforts in this direction parallel those of such European Romantics as Victor Hugo, who attempted to overthrow established physical techniques of painting and substitute for them a witches' brew of self-invented pigments. A dissatisfaction with traditional materials was common to many Romantic artists: these were painters of the enigma who wished to grind their own tones of moonlight, pallor and blood.

When Page returned to America, he settled in New Jersey near the home of his friend, George Inness, who was in certain ways no less a mystic than himself. Like Page, Inness had studied theology and metaphysics though without formal instruction. Except for brief training under Régis Gignoux in New York and a year's apprenticeship as a map engraver, he was a self-taught artist whose style was formed by inborn talent and several trips to Europe, the first in 1847. Inness abandoned his plan to study in Düsseldorf and became a devoted disciple of the Barbizon school. His magnificent early *The Monk* (ill. p. 75) shows the impact of a fifteen months' stay in Rome and for dramatic strength is not to be matched by his later works. But it is these later works, such as *The Approaching Storm* (ill. p. 75), which are the more personal. Their relation to the landscapes of Rousseau and Daubigny is obvious, yet their trembling, soft, atmospheric effect is original and in its way Romantic. The painter sought an almost secret communication with the observer through delicate hints of mood and darkening hour. "A work of art does not appeal to the intellect," he wrote. "It does not appeal to the moral sense. Its aim is not to instruct, not to edify, but to awaken an emotion. Its real greatness consists in the quality and force of this emotion."[45]

2. Hunt, Vedder, La Farge

As Samuel Isham pointed out, the career of William Morris Hunt furnishes many parallels with that of Washington Allston. Both were men of wide knowledge and interest, both occupied key positions in the artistic life of Boston. More important still, both men in their person and work were major factors in the elevation of American art from an insular to an international status. Finally, both paid dearly for their conviction in a new and expanding country, where the strongest currents of creative energy were directed into literary or material channels. Allston's statement that his career might have prospered in Europe is echoed in Hunt's lament: "In another country I might have been a painter!"[46] But probably neither artist repented seriously the decision which had brought him home to live and work.

[44] *Ibid.*, p. 222. [45] McSpadden, *op. cit.*, pp. 123-24.
[46] Helen M. Knowlton, *Art Life of William Morris Hunt*, Boston, 1899, p. 198.

Hunt's early career reveals very clearly the changing focus of American art in the mid-century. He left Harvard to live abroad with his family, turned his back on Düsseldorf after a brief stay, disliked Rome and found in Paris and Barbizon the nerve centers of advanced contemporary figure painting, as Inness found them in landscape. He became the pupil of Couture and afterwards the disciple of Millet. His own art was greatly influenced by both French masters, but he also admired the two key French Romantics, Delacroix and, above all, Géricault, whom he described as "one of the greatest of modern painters"[47] and whom he was said to resemble in appearance. He returned to America in 1855, living first in Newport and, after 1862, in Boston, where his collection of Millets and Baryes helped inaugurate the new taste for French art which spelled the doom of the Düsseldorf vogue. To his pupils he continually railed against the precise technique taught in the Düsseldorf studios. "You see a beautiful sunset," he said, "and a barn comes into your picture. Will you grasp the whole at once in a grand sweep of broad sky and a broad mass of dark building, or will you stop to draw in all the shingles on the barn, perhaps even the nails on each shingle; possibly the shaded side of each nail? Your fine sunset is all gone while you are doing this."[48]

Hunt began to paint late enough in the 19th century so that his art carries few of the literary connotations so common in the work of men like Allston and Cole. He once said: "I like Joy in my studies! and I don't like *literary indigestions!*"[49] He had no faith whatever in a pre-existing Romanticism of subject, and was contemptuous of painters who depended upon mountains to make their pictures impressive. Nevertheless, his art was in certain ways evolved from the Romantic premise of the earlier generations, particularly in its emphasis on force and spontaneity of execution. "You want a picture to seize you as forcibly as if a man had seized you by the shoulder!" he advised his pupils.[50] And he believed that force was arrived at quickly or not at all. He himself painted with extraordinary rapidity, keeping as many as one hundred and fifty bare canvases in his studio so that he could record inspiration of various kinds simultaneously. His *Talks on Art*—transcriptions of verbal advice given his pupils, recorded by one of them—constitute a running tribute to the virtues of spontaneity. His conception of the artist was of a man to whom moments of creative power come fleetingly and must be instantly exploited or lost. In this conception he belongs to the Romantic tradition. Early in the century Byron had compared himself as a poet to the tiger which goes growling back to its lair if it misses its first spring. Some years later Delacroix issued his famous dictum on spontaneity: "If you are not skillful enough to make a sketch of a man throwing himself out of a window, in the time it takes him to fall from the fourth floor to the ground, you will never be able to produce great masterpieces."[51] When Delacroix invited Hunt to

[47] *Ibid.*, p. 66.
[48] W. M. Hunt's *Talks on Art*, First Series, Boston, 1875, pp. 1-2.
[49] *Ibid.*, p. 69.
[50] *Ibid.*, p. 2.
[51] Charles Baudelaire, *La Vie et l'Oeuvre d'Eugène Delacroix*, Paris, 1928, p. 43.

his studio after seeing the latter's *Marguerite* in the Salon of 1852, the two men must have talked with easy sympathy.

Hunt was primarily a studio artist who spent much of his career in his painting rooms at Boston and Magnolia, yet a great number of his pictures were directly derived from objects or scenes which he saw outdoors. Like Mount before him, he had a sketching van constructed, with a studio and bunks, and traveled about in it. From 1874 to the end of his life he painted a number of landscapes, including that inevitable subject for 19th century American artists—Niagara Falls. His masterpiece, the first version of *The Bathers* (ill. p. 72), was inspired by the sight of two boys bathing in the Charles River, one posed to dive from the other's shoulders. The subject was the kind to appeal to a man of Hunt's temperament, since it depicted a split-second of suspended action, never to come again. Hunt was perfectly conscious wherein the subject's charm for him lay. "I don't pretend that the anatomy of this figure is precisely correct," he said of the picture. "In fact, I know it is not. It's a little feminine but I . . . was chiefly occupied with the pose. I *do* think the balancing idea is well expressed, and it is the fear of disturbing that which prevents my making any changes in the figure. I know that I could correct the anatomy, but if the pose were once lost I might never be able to get it again."[52] In another connection he once declared: "A thing that is corrected is like a whipped dog."[53] The premise is as old as Romantic theory itself. In 1714 Pier Jacopo Martelli had insisted that a flaw in a work of art was an indication of its having been created by a superior artist.

Of Hunt's technical procedure full documentation exists in his *Talks on Art*. "Make flat masses of the right value," he said, "and put your care into the edges."[54] As a technician he helped lead American painting away from the tight realism, over-modeling and general literalism of the earlier schools, and his importance in this regard can scarcely be overestimated. But his significance, like that of Allston, is larger than this. He promoted a faith in a vocabulary of expression particular to the art of painting. His pride in medium was salutary in a country whose Anglo-Saxon cultural tradition was heavily overweighted with literature. To Boston in its literary prime he proudly announced: "Painting, only, is worth the while."[55]

One of Hunt's strongest convictions was that only artists could understand art, only artists could teach it. He himself instantly appreciated the talents of Elihu Vedder, and he gave lessons in painting to John La Farge. It was he who persuaded Vedder to exhibit in Boston and thereby launched the career of one of the most puzzling figures in American art. For Vedder, the mystic painter of enigmas, was in person a jocular, extraverted man, whose autobiography contains many anti-Romantic references to his own works and is written in a spirit of rather heavy horseplay, with innumerable references to tavern meetings with the "Boys." Visitors to the studio in Rome

[52] Martha A. S. Shannon, *Boston Days of William Morris Hunt*, Boston, 1923, pp. 127-28.
[53] Knowlton, *op. cit.*, p. 65.
[54] Hunt, *op. cit.*, p. 14.
[55] Knowlton, *op. cit.*, p. 149.

where he worked for eighteen years were invariably startled by the discrepancy in character between the man and his work. The creator of *The Roc's Egg, The Questioner of the Sphinx* and *The Lair of the Sea Serpent* was a man who once described painting as "such a fearful interruption to smoking."[56]

The Lair of the Sea Serpent (ill. p. 69) was painted in 1864, and Vedder asserts: "[I] drew it all out of my own head with a common lead pencil."[57] The "Boys" called the picture "The Big Eel," and McSpadden implies that Vedder freely admitted its model was an ordinary eel. Vedder denies this in his autobiography, yet in writing of his childhood in the same book he says: "When very little I used to be taken over to New Jersey on visits . . . It was there that fishing in a ditch I caught a great eel. I was frightened when I got the great brute out on the grass, for he seemed to my childish eyes a veritable python, and I did not know what to do with him, or how to secure him. . ."[58] The passage testifies to the power of subconscious inspiration based upon childhood experience, even in cases where the artist ignores the role played by such inspiration.

The Lair of the Sea Serpent contributes to a native Romanticism of animals which, as might be expected in a country of vast seaboards, is often concerned with monsters of the deep—the sharks of Copley and Homer, the whales of Ryder and Melville. The painting retains much of the attraction of menace which made it so well known in its day and led James Jackson Jarves to write: "The Lair of the Sea-Serpent fascinates by its oppressive probability of fact." Jarves goes on to draw a distinction between Vedder, who used a realistic technique to make the unbelievable appear plausible, and Gustave Doré, who exaggerated the unlikely. "Doré," wrote Jarves, "appalls the imagination; Vedder alarms the reason, lest these things be so."[59] But Vedder can more profitably be compared to the Swiss Romantic, Arnold Böcklin, whose career began later than his own. Like Böcklin he had inherited a strong sense of Germanic fantasy. Both men lived for long periods in Italy, and both worked along comparable lines in isolation from the prevailing esthetics.

John La Farge, in his *Wolf Charmer* of 1907 (ill. p. 80), also contributed to the Romantic menagerie, but the work was not typical and it would be difficult to imagine two artists more opposite in temperament than himself and Vedder, though the men were friends. While Vedder was a Bohemian artist of limited intellectual range, La Farge was a student of the physical sciences, a talented essayist and lecturer, an art critic who wrote the finest appreciations of Géricault and Delacroix which have yet been published in this country. La Farge was what he appeared to be in his self-portrait painted in 1859 (ill. p. 73): an esthete of exceptionally subtle thought and poetic response, a professional of beauty with an amateur's eclecticism of taste, an easel painter who also worked in stained glass, mosaics, ivory, mother-of-pearl, wood, metal and marble. He was in short a new phenomenon in 19th century American art—an artisan-artist-connoisseur.

[56] Elihu Vedder, *The Digressions of V.*, Boston, 1910, p. 73.
[57] *Ibid.*, p. 264.
[58] *Ibid.*, p. 11.
[59] Jarves, *op. cit.*, p. 249.

Before William Morris Hunt encouraged him to turn professional during the period of their association in Newport in 1859, La Farge had traveled and studied in Europe and had briefly enrolled in Couture's studio to learn painting as a leisure-time accomplishment. It is significant that in Paris he was most deeply affected by the paintings of Chassériau, that ill-fated artist who wavered so long between the schools of Ingres and Delacroix and whose final decision in favor of the latter school was an important indication of Romanticism's final ascendancy. La Farge also saw a few Pre-Raphaelite paintings in England at the Manchester Exposition, and though one critic has declared that he "skirted the Pre-Raphaelite peril,"[60] the influence of the Brotherhood and William Morris was a dominant one throughout most of his career, as he himself admitted. After working under Hunt at Newport, he returned to England and met Ford Madox Brown, William Rossetti and Edward Burne-Jones. Immediately thereafter he went to the Continent to study the technique of stained glass, to which he was to devote so many years. In his conviction that esthetic reform must extend to many media and must be accomplished through the intervention of the individual artist, he was a relatively typical second generation Pre-Raphaelite. And this revivalist conviction was essentially Romantic. It represented a final and practical flowering of the veneration for the Middle Ages which is so basic an ingredient of the Romantic philosophy; it hailed the artist as a universal creator and sanctified both his imagination and his skill.

The search for Romantic subject matter had led certain artists more or less steadily westward during the 19th century, from the Catskills to the Rockies, from New York to Missouri and the Far West. La Farge, whose interest in the Orient had probably been stimulated by Hunt's collection of Japanese prints and by the scholarship of Fenollosa, sailed for Japan in 1886 and somewhat later went to Samoa, the Fiji Islands, Ceylon and Hawaii. (His voyage to the South Seas precedes that of Gauguin by several years.) He thus added in paintings and watercolors to the store of Romantic iconography devoted to the distant-in-place. The spirit in which he did so was far different from that of earlier explorers like Church, but it was still Romantic beneath an outer disguise of pure estheticism.

3. Whistler and Dewing

The estheticism of late century American painting reached its climax in the works and career of this country's most famous artist, James Abbott McNeill Whistler. In fact the art-for-art's-sake dandyism of Whistler's art and person was so pronounced that it has tended to obscure the Romantic aspects of his theories and accomplishment. But, to begin with, he was an artist who believed in that interdependence of the arts which in earlier Romantics had promoted a close alliance between literature and painting and which in his own case promoted one between art and music. He called his pictures symphonies, nocturnes and harmonies, and he thought of them as painted music. He thus stressed the associational impetus of a medium other than his own. And further, Whistler was no less sensitive to the poetry of mood and hour than so unmistakable a Romantic as

[60] Henri Focillon, "John La Farge," *Creative Art—American Magazine of Art*, May, 1936, p. 317.

Ryder. He was often the painter of night, as in *Nocturne in Blue and Silver: the Lagoon, Venice* (ill. p. 73) included in the present exhibition. So much—so much too much—has been written about him that more will not be added here. But he belongs with those Romantics of the late 19th century to whom the passionate emotionalism of the 1830 generation passed, muted and endlessly refined, but basically intact.

Thomas W. Dewing has been dead only five years, yet he seems primarily a 19th century artist, and the works with which we are concerned here were painted before 1900. Perhaps it is the *fin de siècle* spirit of Dewing's works which accounts for the fact that so little has been done lately to commemorate them. Like all artists too intimate with fashion, he has suffered eclipse with the change in general taste which has taken place since the years of his prime. But in his finest works he was a subtle, original and engaging artist who deserves to be reexamined at full length.

Dewing's Romanticism was of a special kind. It consisted in the extraordinary spatial arrangement of certain of his pictures and in their atmospheric content. In *The Recitation* (ill. p. 81), for example, a strange rapport is established between the two figures, and between them and the surrounding empty spaces. The basis of Dewing's compositional economy is certainly to be found in Japanese prints, but to this basis he added a curious intimacy of emptiness, achieved through a soft manipulation of the color and surface of his canvases. His atmosphere creates a Romantic vacuum in which the figures are evocatively suspended. And further to confound reality, he often painted interior scenes as though they were taking place outdoors, while outdoor subjects, such as *The Recitation*, are grouped as if they were happening in a formal drawing room. He used perspective as a metaphysical instrument and for its emotional effect. In the *Girl with Flute* in the collection of the Freer Gallery, the figure is placed with a compositional daring which seems less the result of willful interest in asymmetry than of a kind of dream dictation heeded by the artist.

Most of Dewing's best paintings have the same unreal accord between open space and figures. It is a quality also to be felt in William Morris Hunt's *The Ball Players* (ill. p. 72) and in certain pictures by the contemporary artist, Ben Shahn. But in Dewing's case its effect is heightened by what a critic has called the "physical tenuity" of his figures.[61] This tenuity extends to the still life elements of his paintings, to his fragile furniture and exotic musical instruments, to the general furnishings of his interiors and to his landscapes peopled with chairs. Unaccountably, Dewing's canvases often call to mind the classical paintings of David, but of a David turned elegant, dreamlike and anti-dramatic, of a David turned like himself into a Romantic of hushed space, fine objects and phantoms dressed by the *haute couture.*

4. Eastman Johnson and Winslow Homer

Eastman Johnson is one of the many 19th century American painters who were only incidentally Romantic and that infrequently. A number of his subjects have acquired an extrinsic nostalgic interest over the years since they were painted, notably the Civil War scenes and the long series

[61] Nelson C. White, "The Art of Thomas W. Dewing," *Art and Archeology*, June, 1929, p. 259.

depicting the making of maple syrup in the Maine woods. But Johnson was primarily a portrait and genre artist whose training and inclination led him, during the years from 1859 to 1879, to a realistic story-telling which was often sharp in phrase and eloquently delivered. He had studied in Düsseldorf (1849-51), and thereafter had spent three and one half years in Holland, where he learned that deft handling of bright crosslight through which he may have influenced Winslow Homer. In occasional works, such as the almost Pre-Raphaelite *Girl Picking Water Lilies* (ill. p. 71), he modified the realistic approach within which, it should be noted, he showed considerable imaginative power. Nevertheless, he lacked the intense creative energy which sometimes forced Winslow Homer, protesting bitterly, beyond the borders of realism and into Romanticism proper.

When Winslow Homer was asked whether he ever took liberties in painting his subjects, he replied emphatically: "Never! Never! When I have selected the thing carefully, I paint it exactly as it appears."[62] It would in fact be difficult to think of an American painter who went to such elaborate lengths to assure fidelity of representation. *The Life Line* (1884) was begun only after Homer had made a trip to Atlantic City to learn the intricate handling of the breeches buoy; *The Fog Warning* (1885) was painted from a dingy drawn up on a beach, with a model posed inside; for *The Lookout—All's Well!* (1896) Homer used a clay model of a ship's bell which he himself made after excursions to the junk shops of Boston had failed to turn up the real article. Moreover, it is worth noting that the Romantic drama of suspense in certain of Homer's canvases is pointed up for the spectator by titles which the painter himself had not given the pictures. *The Fog Warning*, for example, was originally called simply *Halibut Fishing*, and under the latter title the plight of the lone fisherman rowing for shore against an oncoming fog is of less unmistakable dramatic interest.

Homer was primarily a realist, and it is with no intention of positive, over-all reclassification that certain Romantic aspects of his painting are here considered. But it is worth noting that after his trip to Tynemouth, England, in 1881, and more particularly after he moved permanently to Prout's Neck, Maine, in 1884, the spirit of his paintings changed in the Romantic direction. His attention to realism of representation, though continued, finds strong precedent in earlier Romantic art, as already noted in connection with Benjamin West. And if we accept as fact that his late career procedure was "To lie in wait for the rare or exceptional phase of nature, and especially the dramatic,"[63] it should be remembered that he sometimes waited a full year for the sea or sun or moonlight to be right for his purpose. The time seems unconscionably long for an artist reputed to be interested only in outer reality. It is tempting to believe that, as in the case of Courbet, Homer's businesslike, anti-esthetic attitude toward his own art was a shield to an underlying warmth and emotionalism. A common phobia among Romantics, from and including Delacroix, has been a dread of the term by which they are known.

[62] John W. Beatty, "Introductory Note," William Howe Downes, *The Life and Works of Winslow Homer*, Boston and New York, 1911, p. xxvii. [63] *Ibid.*, p. xxvi.

During the '80s and '90s, Homer painted a number of canvases which transcend the limits of realism in dramatic content and handling. His *Gulf Stream* (ill. p. 79) was compared by his contemporaries to Géricault's *Raft of the Medusa* and from one viewpoint is more Romantic in that it emphasizes the elemental struggle between nature and man, while Géricault's picture is above all a studio manifesto on a political issue. *The Fox Hunt* (1893) (ill. p. 78) is an unforgettable painting, in which the wheeling attack of the crows establishes a separate animal world of inexorable violence, an accomplishment to which many European Romantics futilely aspired. *Summer Night* (ill. p. 78) with its haunting moonlight and poignant composition, surely deserves high place in American Romantic art. It was painted outdoors at night, as all of Homer's moonlight pictures seem to have been.

No artist's life could have been more prosaic than Homer's. At Prout's Neck, a point of land which his brothers developed into a summer resort without worrying about the effect on Homer's inspiration, he lived a life comparable to that of a shy, retired business man devoted to outdoor recreation. He spoke of his work as the "picture line,"[64] and was little concerned with esthetic matters. Such Romanticism as there was about him was in his art. In this he differed from his contemporaries, Newman, Blakelock and Ryder, all of whom were true Romantics in person as in their painting.

The High Romantic: Newman, Blakelock, Ryder

The earliest of America's three high Romantics was Robert Loftin Newman, born in Richmond, Virginia, and brought up in Tennessee. During his long career Newman had only two public exhibitions of his work; both were in 1894, the first at Knoedler's in New York, the second at the Museum of Fine Arts, Boston. By comparison with Ryder and even with Blakelock, he has remained an obscure artist, though not without a devoted circle, and the reasons usually given for his neglect are that he lived as a recluse and that his paintings are mostly small in size. The second reason is probably the more valid (the fame of both Ryder and Winslow Homer was partly built upon their Romantic status as hermits), for to a 19th century public accustomed to the panoramas of the Hudson River school, largeness of scale was a likely complement to serious attainment. There were few collectors and critics—and they were the ones who bought and encouraged both Newman and Ryder—who realized that the entire Romantic spirit could be encompassed in the fragment or the miniature, that Romanticism was undergoing a reaction against the overstatement of its own earlier period. Though Delacroix was himself one of the most prolific and ambitious Romantics, his charge that Victor Hugo resembled a man of talent who said everything that came into his head, is symptomatic of the change. From the mid-century on, a number of Romantics were content to speak in a smaller but purer voice.

In our own century Newman has remained comparatively unappreciated because of those

[64] William Howe Downes, *The Life and Works of Winslow Homer*, Boston and New York, 1911, p. 167.

very qualities as a Romantic wherein he differs from Ryder. He was not a master of abstract pattern as was Ryder, he painted rapidly and deliberately left a number of his pictures unfinished,[65] and his principal charm lies in his highly professional orchestrations of color and distortions of line (ill. p. 80). It is a charm not to be appreciated at a glance, particularly in an age which expects such painterly emphasis to be accompanied by marked shock value in subject or lack of subject. Newman was an artist who worked within narrow traditional themes, and he is perhaps too close to European Romanticism for chauvinistic comfort.

Newman went abroad in 1850, intending to study in Düsseldorf. Like Hunt, Inness and La Farge he changed his mind and instead went to Paris, where he enrolled in the inevitable studio of Couture. His stay was of short duration, but by 1854 he was back in Paris again and had met Millet through William Morris Hunt. He spent several months as the neighbor and friend of the Barbizon artist, who influenced him strongly toward a simple earthiness of theme, but his true masters were Daumier and Delacroix. His hard, sweeping vigor of line, tenebrous modeling and summary disposition of masses frequently recall Daumier, while in such paintings as *The Attack* (cat. no. 155) the influence of Delacroix is paramount in both subject and handling. The sumptuous coloring of Newman's occasional still lifes of flowers (cat. no. 154) is also reminiscent of the great French Romantic and, through him, of the 16th century Venetians.

For all Newman's affinity to French art, he is an original and rewarding painter and one of the finest technicians in American art. As already noted, his Romanticism speaks a rather professional language. Its dramatic content is minor, its virtues quiet but sure to claim gradually increasing attention. Certain of his defenders have lately hailed him as superior to Ryder, since dark horses can be rescued from their fate only by being allowed to come in first. This praise is far more than he deserves; he hardly belongs in Ryder's rare company.

Ralph Albert Blakelock, in the years just before his death, came into such extraordinary fame that one of his canvases was sold to a museum for $20,000. For this fame and patronage he paid a tragic price: twenty years' incarceration in an asylum for the incurably insane. He was committed in 1899, and gradually the story of his plight became known to art circles, promoting if not actually impelling an interest in his paintings, as in the case of van Gogh. Considered in human terms Blakelock's horrible life evokes the greatest sympathy, and the Romantic creed can have been little comfort to him during his years of nightmare and delusion. But this creed included among its tenets a respect for madness as a divine and mysterious state. From the safe ground of unwavering sanity, even from the closer and more dangerous vantage point of terrifying neuroticism, the Romantics looked upon lunacy as a transforming illness, releasing vast powers of imagination. Now one of their number had experienced it himself. But he left no records to inform his colleagues; all of his paintings were painted before 1899.

[65] The leading authority on Newman writes: "Most of his work appears to have been completed with great spontaneity; a few brush marks and the canvas was completed." (Marchal E. Landgren, "Robert Loftin Newman," *American Magazine of Art*, March, 1935, p. 138.)

These paintings, unlike those of Ryder, are nearly all landscapes. Their compositions were sometimes inspired by such proto-Surrealist sources as the broken enamel in the artist's bathtub, yet these compositions are nearly always organized within conventional formulas. Blakelock was in no sense an innovator in design, as Ryder was, and the interest of his pictures derives almost entirely from his dark and feverish handling of muted color. His best works were inspired by a trip to the Indian territory of the West which he made as a young man. His *Moonlight* (ill. p. 77) illustrates the full range of his accomplishment: a tender vision of the night expressed in earth colors and golden reflections, limited, minor, but informed with its own sincerity of emotion. It is the authenticity of his Romanticism rather than his gifts of imagination and technique which places him in the company of Newman and Ryder.

During the quarter century since Albert Pinkham Ryder's death his name has become synonymous with Romanticism in American painting and for indisputable reason. He was in person the very type of Romantic artist, exalted, solitary, living in constant and fierce communion with his own inner world of imagination, awaiting inspiration as the faithful await miracles and forcing it to its ultimate expression through a figurative "prayer and fasting."[66] In contrast to Hunt, who attacked his canvases impatiently, Ryder spent years finishing some of his pictures. He wrote poems to accompany many of them and after 1900, his inspiration gone, he did nothing but refinish his earlier works in the hope of bringing them nearer perfection. He had an alchemist's reverence for the materials of his trade and a Romantic's contempt for the question of their durability. It was the act of creation which was sacred to him, and when friends told him his canvases were cracking badly he remarked: "When a thing has the elements of beauty from the beginning it cannot be destroyed."[67]

In his rather special mysticism Ryder has several European counterparts—the Englishman, Samuel Palmer, and the Dutchman, Matthew Maris, among others. But in his painting itself he was more individual than any other American artist save possibly Winslow Homer, and it is small wonder that on his two brief trips to Europe he was unaffected by any of the paintings he saw, though he admired the works of Corot and Maris. Fairly early in his mature career he worked out a compositional system which revolved around "three solid masses of form and color—sky, foliage and earth—the whole bathed in an atmosphere of golden luminosity."[68] He varied the system with extraordinary range of effect and developed a contrapuntal disposition of broad areas of sky, cloud and earth which has made him a particular hero to 20th century artists interested in abstract design. (A number of his paintings of seashore coves are as abstract as those of the modern French artist, Georges Braque.) Whether he was painting *Macbeth and the Witches* (ill. p. 82), *The Forest of Arden* (cat. no. 181) or simply one of his numerous sea pictures (ill. p. 84), his dramatic handling

[66] Frederic Fairchild Sherman, *Albert Pinkham Ryder*, New York, 1920, p. 38.
[67] *Ibid.*, p. 43.
[68] *Ibid.*, p. 13.

depended not so much upon incidentals of subject as upon an over-all intensity of expression, an emotive balance of arbitrary yet natural forms. Yet when he needed particularization his imagination was more than adequate; the limp, collapsing boat and the surging whale in his masterwork *Jonah* (ill. p. 83), are proof for the most skeptical. And it should be remembered that each of Ryder's abstract forms carries a distillate of meaning, attained through an endless manipulation of the pigment. Ryder himself was clear on this point. "A daub of white will serve as a robe to Miranda," he wrote.[69] But he immediately adds that it will do so only "if one feels [in it] the shrinking timidity of the young maiden as the heavens pour down upon her their vials of wrath."[70] He felt that paint must be not only color and surface but symbolic magic, and in his devoted hands it often was.

Except for a brief training in New York under William E. Marshall and even less formal training in the school of the National Academy, Ryder was a self-taught artist, as were the majority of American Romantics in the 19th century. Consequently his art and that of certain of his predecessors and contemporaries have a freshness not to be found in countries of longer artistic tradition. He and they were visionaries who fought toward competence in order to release a new, untutored beauty. They lived for the most part in their own imaginations, but they could still hear acutely the sound of the elements against which older civilizations had adopted infinite precautions over the centuries. There were European Romantics of greater genius and accomplishment than Ryder, but none more genuinely—to use his own phrase—"soaked in the moonlight."[71]

The Twentieth Century

Transitional Painters

Of the comparatively few artists Ryder admitted to his studio, one was a painter whose career spanned the transition from 19th to 20th century Romanticism. This was the "Grand Parnassian and Transcendental Eagle of the Arts"—Louis M. Eilshemius. It appears likely that Eilshemius, whose contempt for other living artists was admirably consistent, was least contemptuous of Ryder. He went to the trouble of trying to improve upon the latter's *Macbeth and the Witches* and *Flying Dutchman;* he failed, of course, but not dismally. He was himself a Romantic eccentric of the first order, who once described life as "merely a semblance of a series of nightmares diluted very faintly with a parsimony of shortest delights."[72] He traveled to those five-starred centers of Romantic inspiration, Morocco and Samoa, and did numerous pictures of both countries. And when he stopped painting around 1921 he had explored a wider range of Romantic iconography than perhaps any other American painter—scenes from literature, moonlit nudes, melancholy landscapes, Oriental subjects, stormy sea pieces, scenes of passion and disaster.

[69] *Ibid.*, p. 37. [70] *Ibid.*, p. 37. [71] *Ibid.*, p. 26.
[72] Louis M. Eilshemius, *The Art Reformer*, New York, 1911, vol. II, no. 2, p. 8.

Some indication of this range may be had from the three paintings included in the present exhibition, *Don Quixote* (ill. p. 86), *Afternoon Wind* (cat. no. 84) and *Jealousy* (ill. p. 86). As sometimes happens with artists, his sensualism increased with age, reaching a climax in the extraordinary work, *Jealousy*, with its naive violence, surcharged atmosphere and instinctive precision of compositional balance. Eilshemius brought to Romantic painting an almost inexhaustible fantasy, expressed in a technique which is not yet fully appreciated for its quality or for its suitability to his changing purpose. The influence of Corot seems strongest in his works, though in 1911 the list of artists he considered great contained the disparate names of Titian, Van Dyck, Rubens, Géricault, David, Corodi [sic], Vereshtchagin, Fortuny and Böcklin.[73] To all these artists he romantically preferred himself.

The meeting between Ryder and Eilshemius is said to have taken place in 1908, a crucial date in modern art on many scores. Cubism was launched then, and since that time modern European painting, centered in Paris, has produced formal movements in bewildering succession; two of these movements, Surrealism (1924) and Neo-Romanticism (1926), have been predominantly Romantic in approach. American painting over the same period has been by comparison a matter of individual direction, and its artists of Romantic tendency have usually painted in spiritual isolation, without benefit of manifestoes or organized and continuous performances on an agreed theme. Thus the group of painters which in 1908 opened the path for modern art in this country was known characteristically as "The Eight."[74] The group consisted of artists who, finding themselves more closely allied in friendship than in belief, formed their title by the antidoctrinal expedient of counting noses. They were an assorted lot, and the most Romantic of them was Arthur B. Davies, whose soft, decorative, idyllic style continued the tradition of the early La Farge and paid homage to the Renaissance masters, particularly Giorgione. Davies' *Dream* (ill. p. 85), portraying a somnambulist figure in a landscape out of Odilon Redon, is obviously, perhaps too obviously, within the Romantic province and not unrelated to Eilshemius' *Afternoon Wind* in its atmospheric poesy. *Along the Erie Canal* (ill. p. 85) is an elegiac and delicate transformation of nature into a playground for otherworldly children. Both paintings illustrate Davies' Romanticism of innocence and sweet aspiring.

Romantic Realism

Davies' Romanticism created a dulcet irreality. That of the painters now to be considered sprang from reality itself—reality so projected as to reveal a Romantic appeal which had passed unnoticed in the failing light of constant usage. These painters celebrated the contemporary scene, as Romantic artists had done increasingly since the mid-19th century, and thereby helped confute

[73] Eilshemius, *op. cit.*, vol. II, no. 1, page 7.
[74] Davies, Glackens, Henri, Lawson, Luks, Prendergast, Shinn and Sloan.

Samuel Palmer's blunt premise: "The past for poets, the present for pigs."[75] John Sloan, a member of "The Eight," in such paintings as *The City from Greenwich Village* (ill. p. 88) interpreted New York with love and transforming devotion, and was one of the founders of a street scene Romanticism which continues to flourish among both painters and photographers. George Bellows, though his *The Picnic* (ill. p. 87) is in the pastoral style of Davies, and though his illustrations for the novels of Donn Byrne and H. G. Wells are purely imaginative, was more often a Romantic Realist. His paintings and lithographs of actual prize fights (ill. p. 87) are in an opposite mood from Davies' work and revert to that emotionalism of violent physical action of which the 19th century prophet was Théodore Géricault.[76] But for Géricault and his French contemporaries boxing had been an aristocratic sport imported from England and reserved for the few. In America and in Bellows' period it was the people's spectacle and an outlet for group emotion, supported and promoted by a press which to this day has made its sport pages the last refuge of an unabashedly romantic prose.

As already noted in connection with Blakelock, madness deeply impressed certain artists of the early 19th century, and Bellows' fine print, *Dance in a Madhouse* (cat. no. 19), combines the Romantic appeal of insanity with that of the frenzied physical action mentioned above. Of this action Rockwell Kent early in the century became a well-known protagonist in both his life and his art. An explorer and traveler, he turned to the North countries, whose winter Romanticism of ice and snow had attracted Church sixty years before. In his person he furnished that glamor of hardihood and brave adventuring which is never entirely free of Romantic connotation. In his art the Romantic Realism of his early sea pieces in oil (ill. p. 88) eventually gave way to the stylized idealism of his woodcuts, which watered Blake's mystic potions to popular strength.

In 1924 Edward Hopper exhibited his watercolors in New York, and the success of the exhibition led him after years of discouragement to work again in oils, a medium in which he has since shown steadily increasing mastery. Of his own work Hopper has written: "My aim in painting has always been the most exact transcription possible of my most intimate impressions of nature."[77] For our purposes it is the word "intimate" which is crucial in this definition. Like Winslow Homer, Hopper is ostensibly a realist, intent upon a direct and forceful transcription of appearances, without alterations either Romantic or Classic. His horizontal system of composition is simplicity itself; his subjects are everywhere in America, for everyone to see. But it is the intimacy of Hopper's impressions of the obvious which carries him into Romanticism, and this intimacy is of a dramatic and thoroughly personal kind. In *Gas* (color plate opposite), for example, there is no willful transformation of the scene, no aid to literary association, yet there is the loneliness of the

[75] John Piper, *British Romantic Artists*, London, 1942, p. 31.

[76] One of Géricault's finest lithographs portrays a match between a white and a Negro boxer, a theme adopted by Bellows. Apart from its exotic implications, the opposition of black figure to white affords the same emphasis on dramatic chiaroscuro which endeared the piebald horse to the Italian masters of the Baroque.

[77] *Edward Hopper, Retrospective Exhibition*, Museum of Modern Art, New York, 1933, p. 17.

Edward HOPPER: Gas. 1940. Oil, 26¼ x 40¼". The Museum of Modern Art, New York.

highways at night, the weird relation of road to surrounding thick woods, the magic tonal opposition of the gas station light to the evening gloom. The picture is blunt fact. It is also realism brought to such a degree of perception that it becomes a Romantic sorcery, seen in a crystal, crystal clear.

Occasionally in recent paintings Hopper has allowed himself a more overt display of emotional participation, as in *Shakespeare at Dusk* (cat. no. 105), with its lyricism of mood and subtle capture of twilight sky over New York. Occasionally he has permitted himself the luxury of an inherently expressive subject, as in *Cape Cod Evening* (ill. p. 89).[78] Whereas dramatic incident is usually reduced in his paintings to the flutter of a window curtain (in an earlier time Hopper might have been known, respectfully be it understood, as "The Master of the Window Curtain"), here the dog in the pathless grass, the watching woman and man, contribute what is almost a plot to the picture. But it is the darkness of ground beneath the woods, the monotony of grass, the decorative richness of the house in this far isolation, which create the painting's essential mystery. Hopper is primarily a poet of the inanimate in figures as well as in landscape and architecture. In his painting, as in the early art of his Italian contemporary, Giorgio de Chirico, the frenzied motion of much early 19th and early 20th century Romanticism comes to an abrupt and slightly uneasy repose. Whereas the Romanticism of Géricault and Bellows often celebrated strident action, that of de Chirico and Hopper depicts a silent, expressionless waiting.

Though Hopper once wandered unmoved amid the fantastic scenery of the Southwest, finally producing a watercolor of a locomotive which might equally well have been painted in New York, the Rio Grande country of New Mexico has proved continuously inspiring to Georgia O'Keeffe. She returns there year after year and there has painted some of her outstanding works. Her *Black Cross, New Mexico* (ill. p. 90) and *Deer's Skull and Pedernal* (cat. no. 159) are essentially Romantic paintings, devoted to a still-life metaphysics which, though deeply personal in style, is technically related to the confessional realism of the German Nazarenes and the English Pre-Raphaelites. Her crisp, flat handling of pigment parallels that of such precisionists as Charles Sheeler, the later Demuth and Preston Dickinson, but is used to tell secrets of psychic response rather than to record the glossy externals of a mechanical age. She uses with exceptional acumen the ancient Romantic device of the fragment to suggest the whole. In *Ranchos Church No. 3* (cat. no. 158), for example, the structure of the entire church and its landscape setting is evoked by a condensed placing of fragmentary forms. Whereas earlier Romantics like Cole and Bierstadt had suggested the monumental through panoramas, O'Keeffe seeks it by placing the spectator in an enchanted, near corner, limiting his view to intensified essentials. Her method is reversed by such younger painters of the Southwest as Peter Hurd and Vance Kirkland, who again paint the West as mountainous and vast.

[78] Hopper prefers the title *Cape Cod Evening* to its story-telling alternate, *Whippoorwill*, just as Winslow Homer preferred *Halibut Fishing* to *The Fog Warning*.

Romantic Expressionism

As early as 1913 John Marin was striving toward a Romantic Expressionism—if, indeed, all Expressionism is not by definition Romantic. In the foreword to his exhibition of that year Marin wrote: "In life all things come under the magnetic influence of other things; the bigger assert themselves strongly, the smaller not so much, but still they assert themselves, and though hidden they strive to be seen and in so doing change their bent and direction. While these powers are at work pushing, pulling, sideways, downwards, upwards, I can hear the sound of their strife and there is great music being played."[79] Considering that this passage describes Marin's reaction to inanimate subject matter—the buildings of New York City—there can be little doubt of the artist's anti-realist temperament. In watercolor Marin has since developed a technique whose essence is emotional force, quickly and directly achieved. The fierce energy of sky in *Sunset, Casco Bay* (ill. p. 91) is the work of a visionary for whom Expressionism has been a natural language. The Cubist angulation of outer forms in *Lower Manhattan* (cat. no. 137) and *On Morse Mountain, Small Point, Maine* (cat. no. 138) is used for organizational effect but also, and perhaps primarily, as a means of sharpening the central impression of the subject, as a diamond is cut to lead light to the heart of the stone. Though Marin was trained to be an architect, he is a painter of mirages rather than symmetrical order. Yet these mirages are cast by nature and retain much of her image. Marin was within the tradition of nature Romanticism founded here by Thomas Cole when he wrote: "Seems to me that the true artist must perforce go from time to time to the elemental big forms—Sky, Sea, Mountain, Plain—and those things pertaining thereto, to sort of re-true himself up, to recharge the battery. For these big forms have everything. But to express these, you have to love these, to be part of these in sympathy."[80]

Both Max Weber and Marsden Hartley have been primarily Expressionist Romantics. Both belonged with Marin to the group of artists which succeeded "The Eight" as the protagonists of revolution in modern American art, though Weber's part in this revolution was earlier and greater than Hartley's. They exhibited with Marin, Alfred H. Maurer and Arthur Dove at Alfred Stieglitz's gallery, "291," in March, 1910, and formed a left wing to the assault on academic standards led by Davies and Henri which reached its climax in the Armory show of 1913. But the works of Weber and Hartley with which we are concerned here were painted only a very short time ago, and both artists have been remarkable for the sustained creative power they have shown in an age when premature collapse of such power has been depressingly frequent. They seem more Romantic in these recent pictures than in those of their youth. Weber's *Winter Twilight* (ill. p. 92) is in the tradition of "ruined" landscape, with bare foreground trees. His *Chassidic Dance* (ill. p. 92) is a whirlpool of figures and flung gestures, Expressionist in technique, but

[79] Herbert J. Seligmann, ed., *Letters of John Marin*, New York, 1931, pp. 2–3.
[80] *John Marin*, Museum of Modern Art, New York, 1936, p. 20.

Romantic in its violent chaos of motion. It is a picture which Delacroix, the painter of the *Convulsionaries of Tangiers*, might have stopped to admire.

Hartley's *Evening Storm, Schoodic, Maine* (ill. p. 93) is organized according to Ryder's basic principle of "three solid masses of form and color," and its abstract patterns of sky and clouds suggest the influence of the 19th century Romantic, whom Hartley knew well and admired profoundly. But Hartley, unlike Ryder, was a magician of summary brushwork, and it is this fact which relates him to Expressionism. The thundering immediacy of *Evening Storm* is near the spirit of Winslow Homer, but more abruptly and emotionally managed. It is a different matter from Ryder's slow alchemy, yet the two artists were allied in fundamental approach, and Hartley's statement on Ryder applied equally to himself: "I have known [in Ryder] that wisdom which is once and for all wisdom for the artist, that confidence and trust that for the real artist there is but one agency for the expression of self in terms of beauty, the eye of the imagination, that mystical third somewhere in the mind which transposes all that is legitimate to expression."[81]

The religious intensity of certain of Weber's paintings is a comparatively rare quality in contemporary art, but a quieter, more restrained sentiment is to be found in the *Fisherman* (ill. p. 94) by the Oregon artist, C. S. Price. Price, a contemporary of Marin, has arrived at a mature and consistent style only in fairly recent years, after a long period of extremely conscientious experiment. His square blocking of forms probably derives from his interest in abstract painting, which he practices upon occasion, yet suggests a definite relationship with the angular style of the German Expressionist, Carl Hofer. The appeal of Price's own paintings is above all Expressionist Romantic, proceeding from the richly worked pigment and resultant rough sincerity of his compositions.

In contrast to the daylight Expressionism of Marin but allied to the murky handling of Price's *Fisherman*, Benjamin Kopman has created an Expressionism of mournful mood and night, of which *A Lynching* (ill. p. 95) is a good example. Much of the latter picture's impact is due to the conviction with which its social commentary is stated, as is the case with Gropper's *The Defenders* (ill. p. 95). This kind of commentary is conspicuously absent in George Grosz's *Early Moon* (cat. no. 98), though Grosz was once among the most brilliant and savage satirists in Europe. The fevered mood of this Cape Cod landscape relates it to that introspective variety of German Expressionism which stirred the still earth to a whirlpool in which man's inner torment was mirrored.

The Romantic Expressionist tendency continues to flourish among younger artists. Donald Forbes paints a millstone as if it were a fragment from Stonehenge, an object for wonder and riveted attention, lying huge in a Romantic gloom and isolation (ill. p. 99). Hyman Bloom's painting carries strong vestiges of his Latvian birth and ancestry; its turbulent Expressionism is similar to that of the Lithuanian, Chaim Soutine, in racial intensity and Baltic splendor of color.

[81] Marsden Hartley, "Albert P. Ryder," *The Seven Arts*, May, 1917, p. 95.

The Skeleton (cat. no. 30) is in the vein of traditional macabre Romanticism as to subject, but it and *The Bride* (ill. p. 99) are primarily abstract labyrinths of color and interlaced forms, nervous, sensitive and strangely evocative of emotion. The Expressionist direction is followed in Joseph De Martini's mildly Romantic self-portrait (ill. p. 98). In Everett Spruce's *The Hawk* (cat. no. 188) the thick impasto and broad modeling, so common in Expressionist technique, are again applied to a rugged daylight subject.

A Romantic Cubist

Lyonel Feininger, despite his fourteen years as an instructor in the German Bauhaus and his devotion to Cubist forms, has always revealed in his paintings a decided poetic preoccupation. *The Steamer Odin* (ill. p. 100), for example, is the record of a mood as well as of mechanical appearances. In its strange mystery of horizon, ghostly lighting and still atmosphere, it is no less a Romantic work than many more representational pictures; it as strongly suggests the hushed drama of the docks at night. This fact seems less surprising when one remembers that Feininger has long admired the German Romantic, Caspar David Friedrich, some of whose compositions he has adapted to his own Cubist vocabulary.

The "Gothick"

Perhaps the most concentrated, consistent and pure manifestation of Romanticism in 20th century American art is to be found in the watercolors which Charles Burchfield executed between the years 1916 and 1918. The existence of these watercolors is in itself a Romantic phenomenon, for they were painted by a very young man living and working in Salem, Ohio, in more or less complete isolation from contemporary esthetic currents and in almost total ignorance of the European Romantic tradition. Certain of these pictures, such as *The Night Wind* (cat. no. 40) and *Church Bells Ringing—Rainy Winter Night* (ill. p. 103), are primarily Expressionist in approach and recreate in visual forms the sensations and alarms of Burchfield's childhood reactions to the elements. But even these are marked by a macabre Romanticism which relates them to the "Gothick" tradition brought to this country by Washington Allston. They are complemented by a group of watercolors, including *The First Hepaticas* (ill. p. 102) and *Garden of Memories* (cat. no. 38), in which the artist has recorded more literary Romantic visions of melancholy and malaise.

There is in nearly all Burchfield's works of this period so clear an impetus of Romantic revelation that they must rank among the most individual manifestations of the Romantic spirit produced in this century and country. Their influence has been considerable. The menacing Expressionism of the first group has been adopted by several painters older and younger than Burchfield. The "Gothick" Romanticism of the second group recurs in Morris Kantor's *Haunted House* (ill. p. 104), Aaron Bohrod's *Tourist House* (ill. p. 106) and in Philip Evergood's *My*

Forebears Were Pioneers (ill. p. 107), though tempered in the last-named case by a humorous detachment on the artist's part. In the same spirit Hobson Pittman has evolved a personal art largely devoted to haunted interiors and gardens, as in *Old Friends* (ill. p. 105) and *The Widow* (cat. no. 169). The spiky, tapering style of his drawing is used to considerable effect to produce an atmosphere of polite spookiness and uneasy elegance.

The "Gothick" novel, as is well known, was converted to contemporary terms by Henry James in *The Turn of the Screw*, a book in which psychological innuendo became the instrument of terror, replacing those physical contrivances of action and scenery upon which the 18th and 19th century writers had depended. In 1918 Charles Demuth completed five watercolors (ill. p. 101) which were apparently intended as interpretations of James' story rather than as direct illustrations to be published in conjunction with the text. The following year he finished three watercolors on the theme of James' *Beast in the Jungle.* All eight works recapture with exceptional acuteness the unspoken suspense and frightfulness of James' two masterpieces, and are fine Romantic art in their own right.

Lyric Painting

In both figure painting and landscape the lyric tradition, followed in the 19th century by such varied artists as Allston, Inness and La Farge, has been continued by painters of the 20th. Bernard Karfiol's *Boy* (ill. p. 112), painted in 1924, is one of the earliest of the brooding Romantic figures which artists like John Carroll and Henry Varnum Poor were later to paint.[82] Both Carroll and Poor have done sensitive portraits illustrating the shy charm of children entering adolescence (ill. p. 114)—that period of life which the late 18th century Romantics held sacred and of which the boy poet, Thomas Chatterton, became the universal martyr-hero. Alexander Brook at one time painted figure pieces influenced by the Spanish Mannerism of Picasso's Rose period, as in *The Tragic Muse* (ill. p. 115). He has since progressed to a more individual art of marked technical control and poetic charm. He now alternates between figure painting and landscape, and in both categories shows an easy freshness. His *Pasture at Elk* (ill. p. 115) combines the atmospheric Romanticism of a George Inness with a deliberate lyricism of subject in which a ruined locomotive is substituted for the bare trees of the Hudson River school. The substitution points up the tendency of modern Romanticism to direct its nostalgia away from eternal nature toward that which was recently made by man and is now outmoded—the Mansard houses of Burchfield and Hopper, the derelict automobiles of Elizabeth Sparhawk-Jones.

The open romanticizing of architectural subjects to which certain painters turned in the 1930s is exemplified by Morris Kantor's *South Truro Church* (cat. no. 120). These painters were following the lead of Burchfield and Hopper, whose watercolors of the mid-1920s had often dealt

[82] The lethargic, introspective mood of Karfiol's figure piece was a persistent factor in the style of the Parisian Neo-Romantic artists, though there was certainly no cross-influence between them and Karfiol.

with Victorian architecture. But whereas the latter two artists had dramatized their subjects through strong lighting which emphasized the forlorn, brave fantasy of such houses, the artists of the 1930s were more deliberately Romantic. For example, Hopper had painted the early 19th century church at South Truro several years before Kantor. He had portrayed the subject objectively, in clear sunlight, while Kantor's version is enveloped in an abstract half-light which creates a subjective mood.

The tendency toward an atmospheric Romanticism is felt in numerous paintings of the past ten years, in the portraits of Carroll and Brook, in Karl Zerbe's shimmering, strange *Terror* (ill. p. 96) and in Arnold Blanch's superbly dreamy *Suwannee River* (ill. p. 116). In all these cases, however, the handling of atmosphere is naturalistic by comparison with Kantor's abstract usage, and reverts to that soft manipulation of tremulous light and air of which George Inness was the most consistent 19th century practitioner.

Lyric Romanticism has attracted a number of painters of a still younger generation. Julian Levi has developed a quiet but extremely agreeable poetry of the seashore in such paintings as *Buoys* (ill. p. 113). His art is comparable to that of the Parisian Neo-Romantic, Léonid Berman, though arrived at independently. Eugene Ludins' pictures appear at casual glance to be matter-of-fact and primarily notable for their skillful naturalism. But he is a subtle fantasist as well. The strange activities of the foreground figures in *Interlude* (ill. p. 117), the mysterious, endless pipe from which emerges a black dog—these suggest a bewitched countryside whose inhabitants have stepped from the pages of a Washington Irving.

The Ryder Tradition

Throughout his mature career Henry Mattson has sacrificed the recognition which comes from being definably "modern," and has remained a thorough Romantic in the 19th century tradition which reached its climax in this country in the art of Ryder. Mattson's recent *Jungle Play* (ill. p. 109) is a Delacroix subject. As such it would have been unpopular with the *avant garde* of the 1920s and 1930s, which had become accustomed to the gunplay of contemporary esthetic revolt and knew that Delacroix's Romanticism was never even remotely the issue. But Mattson is not the first important American artist to have ignored the main direction of art in his time, nor would he be the first in so doing to arrive by shortcut at a destination which a later generation approves. Romanticism appears to be a growing force in American art, though still scattered in effect, and Mattson's fine *Stars and Sea* (ill. p. 108) may yet link Ryder's sea pieces to a more general revival of Romantic subject matter and treatment.

In continuing the Romanticism of night and mystery developed by Ryder, Mattson has not worked alone. The California artist, Matthew Barnes, within the past ten years has produced a number of paintings comparable in viewpoint. But whereas Mattson is a professional painter of long experience and great technical dexterity, Barnes is a self-taught artist. His technique is crude but nevertheless eloquent for his purpose. Like Ryder and Mattson he has worked within a restricted iconography; nearly all of his paintings are of the same obsessive chimera whose symbolic properties are ghostly houses, unlikely hills and streets, lumpy phantoms running inexplicable errands, and over all the moonlight. *High Peak* (ill. p. 111), *Night Scene* (cat. no. 14) and *Ghost Homes* (cat. no. 16) illustrate with what untiring conviction he has rearranged these properties in each new canvas. He has recently worked away from his earlier overdependence on Ryder (and in special instances on Hartley) and has emerged as an independent artist, one of the few to learn to speak in middle age the Romantic language of youth.

Ryder's perennial influence reappears in the patterned chiaroscuro of Elliot Orr's *Desecration* (ill. p. 110). His tenebrous atmosphere has been adopted by Paul Mommer in *At Night* (ill. p. 109) and *The Betrayal* (cat. no. 148), though Mommer's Romanticism is far less cosmic than Ryder's, its emotion deliberately nearer the surface as in the Expressionist works of Kopman.

Regionalism

During the 18th and 19th centuries Romanticism was continually being related by its adherents to a given locale. The Roman campagna, the English Lakes, the Rhine, the American Catskills and Rockies—all became centers of Romantic activity and provided a regionalist faith for their particular enthusiasts. In our own century, as many remember, a regionalist philosophy was revived in the early 1930s in Missouri and Kansas and found its prophet in the eloquent isolationist, Thomas Craven. The philosophy took an extreme form. Whereas earlier regionalism had segregated certain areas as Romantic Meccas open to all and had actually touted for trade, the recent variety adopted more snobbish standards of admission. It declared that artists must derive inspiration from an intimate and continuous association with the place of their birth or very early adoption; further, that this inspiration should express itself in terms of a local realism. For centuries certain great painters have exemplified this premise in their works. But the fact remains that other equally great artists have worked in foreign lands, in sections of their own countries remote from their birthplaces, or in international art centers. It is the stubborn denial of this historical truth, together with the bully-boy, xenophobic and almost secessionist temper in which Midwestern regionalism was conducted ten years ago, that made its propaganda so perverse and inflated.

Perhaps the artists themselves were not to blame for this, and a number of them have produced pictures which are of considerable interest. Thomas Benton's *Moonlight on the Osage* (ill. p. 119) is an orthodox Romantic work, calculated and self-conscious, but more likely to assure him posterity's attention than his murals. John Steuart Curry's *Hogs Killing a Rattlesnake* (ill. p. 119) is a forceful, original example of animal Romanticism and has the plausibility of daily incident on the Kansas farmlands. Because of its intense localism it escapes responsibility for the serious charge which must be brought against the recent regionalism as a whole: that while claiming to free American art from European domination, it often merely changed the source of this influence from the French 19th and 20th centuries to the Flemish 15th century (Grant Wood) or to the Mannerist-Baroque period in Italy (Benton).

The International Tradition

Since the beginning of art in this country certain American painters have worked in particularly close relation to foreign traditions, among them West, Trumbull, Allston, Page, Hunt, La Farge and Whistler. In our own century Davies, Marin, Weber and Hartley have all for varying intervals of their careers been caught up in international currents in painting and taken their impetus from contemporary art abroad or from the great European traditions of the past. A comparable internationalism is a distinguishing mark among the artists now to be considered.

The first of these is Franklin Watkins, an artist of decided ability and heartening ambition. The shock—the pleasant shock—caused by the appearance of his *Suicide in Costume* (ill. p. 120) in 1931 and his *Soliloquy* (ill. p. 121) the following year is still memorable. After a decade of painting in which abstraction and the American Scene were predominating forces, here suddenly was a vigorous, proud, elegant and imaginative art in the grand manner. Coming on the heels of Marin's impulsive *plein-airisme*, following closely Hopper's concentration on American reality, Watkins' painting was a studio art, using the rich devices of the Mannerist and Baroque figure styles. Though its relation to European tradition was obvious, at its best it was a solid, original and courageous accomplishment. Whereas painters like Marin had founded their esthetic upon the consecutive release of quick impressions, Watkins helped revive the individual painting as the summary of a relatively long experience on the artist's part. This is not to say that his accomplishment was greater than that of his predecessors, but that it was rewardingly different. Nor has he foundered on a single, obsessive theme as Allston did in *Belshazzar's Feast*. The very range of his Romanticism has been impressive; it extends from the melodrama of *Suicide in Costume* to the witching melancholia of *Soliloquy*, and thence to the "Gothick" mood of *Rocky Coast* (cat. no. 202).

The individual painting as the summary of considerable experience and accumulated imagery is exemplified, too, in Edwin W. Dickinson's impressive work, *Figures and Still Life* (ill. p. 123), begun in 1933 and completed in 1937. The artist himself has furnished no concise interpretation of its iconography. Its general effect is that of a well furnished studio exploded into disorder, as if Géricault's *Raft of the Medusa* had struck a mine while it was being painted. But this violence has been wreaked by Dickinson's own Romantic imagination, and with infinite care despite the unfinished state of the composition. It would be difficult to think of another modern canvas in which a Grand Style theme has been so painstakingly built up, only to find its true grandeur in an unacademic and mysterious state of ruin.

Elizabeth Sparhawk-Jones pays tribute to Tiepolo in *Lady Godiva* (ill. p. 121), an engaging work which transcends dependence upon its stylistic source. Jon Corbino's *Stampeding Bulls* (ill. p. 122) is in the Rubens-Géricault tradition of furious action and is of interest primarily as an attempt—perhaps too faithful an attempt—to revive the Baroque compositional strategem. Within the last ten years a few younger American artists have evolved a Neo-Baroque figure and landscape painting, based in part upon 17th century models, in part upon the contemporary Neo-Romanticism of Christian Bérard and Eugene Berman. Among these American artists are Richard Blow (ill. p. 125), Edward Melcarth and Walter Stuempfig (ill. p. 124). All three have produced honest and handsome pictures, though theirs is an art which appeals most to those who love its sources, enjoy being reminded of them and like to believe that they are coming to life again (as who can say they may not?). In Raymond Breinin's *The Cloak* (ill. p. 125) the American flavor of Stuempfig's *Dalliance at Cape May* is replaced by a style more closely related to Italian Mannerism or that of El Greco.

Rico Lebrun was born in Italy and lived there until he was twenty-four, hence his Baroque style seems more deeply rooted than that of the artists just mentioned. He is one of the most finished draftsmen of the younger generation, though not necessarily among the most expressive. In recent years he has been absorbed in interpreting the terrors of bombing, which he remembers from firsthand experience in the Italian army of the First World War. He has portrayed the desperate epileptic energy which cripples can summon to flee hospitals under attack (ill. p. 122). In subjects of peace as of war he is above all interested in extremes of tension, physical and emotional, and in this predilection he seems altogether Romantic. Géricault's taste for the violence and horror of butcher shops is echoed in Lebrun's drawings and paintings of the slaughter houses of Southern California.

There is a considerable group of young American artists whose work is related to European Surrealism. Thus John Atherton's *Foggy Day* (ill. p. 124) adopts the incongruous juxtaposition of unlikely objects which formed so important a part of Surrealist procedure. In this particular painting the inclusion of the antique sculpture seems a conscious and rather unsuccessful conceit, lacking the true Surrealist air of irrational compulsion. But the painting of the architecture, figures and rainy sky is masterly, and it should be noted that Atherton has since proceeded to a more direct and convincing interpretation of his subjects, while retaining a hyper-clarity of technique which goes beyond acute observation to Romantic reappraisal. Also within the wider Surrealist orbit, Arthur Osver's *Melancholy of a Rooftop* (ill. p. 125), with its long shadows, black arches and towering chimney, owes much to the pictures of Giorgio de Chirico's early period. Its Romantic treatment contrasts vividly with the realism Charles Sheeler and Preston Dickinson applied to similar scenes twenty years earlier.

Romantics of the Subconscious

In describing his technical procedure Darrel Austin has written: "I size my canvas and then apply the paint, usually with no preconceived idea of subject matter."[83] Though Austin disclaims interest in the work of other artists past or present, his conception of the painter as the agent of a spontaneous, subconscious inspiration is rooted in earlier Romantic philosophy and is the basis of contemporary Surrealism. Following the dictates of such inspiration, Austin has created a rich, if somewhat narrow, mythology of eerie animals and landscapes. He molds the heavy impasto of his canvases into a phosphorescent domain for the creatures of a wholly Romantic imagination (ill. p. 128).

Loren MacIver is more truly the recorder of subconscious inspiration than Austin, and her art shows less formalizing interference on the part of conscious thought. A subtle and varied colorist, she is an impressionist of poetic recognition, capturing the secrets of rare childhood and adult responses and projecting them as an abstract gossamer (ill. p. 127).

To use his own phrase, Morris Graves is a painter of the "inner eye,"[84] that third eye somewhere in the mind, to which Marsden Hartley referred in describing Ryder. Through this inner eye Graves has beheld the lunar visions of *Snake and Moon* (cat. no. 93), *Blind Bird* (color frontispiece) and *Owl of the Inner Eye* (ill. p. 126). Through it he has seen *Little Known Bird of the Inner Eye* (cat. no. 95), which affords a striking comparison with Ryder's *Dead Bird* (ill. p. 84). For while Ryder's picture is an interpretation of external reality, however personal and Romantic this interpretation may be, Graves' painting is complete improvisation. With Graves, as with the late Paul Klee, Romanticism arrives at an interior, symbolic expression, inventing a language of signs and omens to describe an intimate communion between the artist's innermost imagination and his medium. The ectoplasmic scribble within which Graves' figures take shape is related to Mark Tobey's "white writing," utilized by the latter in a number of his works with deliberately mystic intent. Graves freely acknowledges his debt to the older artist, but he is himself perhaps the most consistent young American exponent of that doubly introspective Romanticism for which precedent may be found from the 16th to the 19th centuries but which has reached its widest application in the past twenty years. Among younger men, such as the startlingly talented William Fett (ill. p. 126), this kind of Romanticism still appears to be gaining converts. Graves speaks for himself and for them when he declares: "I paint to rest from the phenomena of the external world."

JAMES THRALL SOBY

[83] *Americans 1942*, Museum of Modern Art, New York, 1942, p. 11.
[84] *Ibid.*, p. 51.

COPLEY: Watson and the Shark. 1778. Oil, 72⅛ x 90¼". Museum of Fine Arts, Boston.

TRUMBULL: The Sortie from Gibraltar (2nd version). 1788. Oil, 20 x 30″. Cincinnati Art Museum.

opposite above: WEST: Saul and the Witch of Endor. 1777. Oil, 20 x 26″. Private collection.

opposite below: WEST: Death on the Pale Horse. 1802. Oil, 21 x 36″. Philadelphia Museum of Art.

ALLSTON: The Deluge. 1804. Oil, 48 x 65¾". Metropolitan Museum of Art.

opposite above: ALLSTON: Moonlit Landscape. c. 1827. Oil, 24 x 35." Museum of Fine Arts, Boston. *Not in the exhibition.*

opposite below: ALLSTON: Diana and Her Nymphs in the Chase. 1805. Oil, 66¼ x 97¾." Collection Mrs. Algernon Coolidge.

COLE: The Expulsion from Eden. 1828. Oil, 39 x $53\frac{3}{4}$". Private collection.

COLE: The Oxbow (Connecticut River near Northampton). 1836. Oil, 51½ x 76″. Metropolitan Museum of Art.

MORSE: The Chapel of the Virgin at Subiaco. 1830–31. Oil, 30 x 37". Worcester Art Museum.

DURAND: Kindred Spirits [Thomas Cole and William Cullen Bryant]. 1849. Oil, 45 x 36″. New York Public Library.

QUIDOR: The Money Diggers. 1832. Oil, 16¾ x 21½″. Collection Mrs. Sheldon Keck.

AUDUBON: Barn Owl. 1833. Aquatint colored by hand. 33¾ x 22⅞". Weyhe Gallery.

AUDUBON: Canada Lynx. 1845. Colored lithograph, 21⅜ x 27⅛". Kennedy & Co.

CATLIN: Ha-wón-je-tah, the One Horn; First Chief of the tribe; Mee-ne-cow-e-gee band, upper Missouri [Sioux (Dah-co-ta)]. c. 1832. Oil, 27⅞ x 23″. United States National Museum, Washington.

Alfred J. MILLER: Buffalo Hunt. c. 1840. Oil, 30 x 44″. Collection Victor D. Spark.

BINGHAM: Daniel Boone Escorting a Band of Pioneers into the Western Country. c. 1851. Oil, 37 x 50″. Washington University, St. Louis.

BINGHAM: Fur Traders Descending the Missouri. c. 1845. Oil, 29¼ x 36¼″. Metropolitan Museum of Art.

CURRIER & IVES: The Life of a Hunter. A Tight Fix. 1861. Colored lithograph, after painting by A. F. Tait; 18¾ x 27″. Collection Harry T. Peters.

CURRIER & IVES: The Lightning Express Trains. Leaving the Junction. 1863. Color lithograph by F. F. Palmer; 17⅞ x 27⅞″. Collection Harry T. Peters.

Artist unknown: Meditation by the Sea. 1860–65. Oil, 13¾ x 19½″. Private collection.

Artist unknown: Buffalo Hunter. 19th century. Oil, 40⅝ x 51½″. Collection Mr. and Mrs. Buell Hammett.

above: MOUNT: Landscape with Figures. 1851. Oil, 19 x 28¼″. Pennsylvania Academy of the Fine Arts.

left: Lilly M. SPENCER: Reading. 1852. Oil, 50⅜ x 37⅞″. Collection Victor D. Spark. *New title.*

opposite above: Robert S. DUNCANSON: Blue Hole, Flood Waters, Little Miami River. 1851. Oil, 29¼ x 42¼″. Cincinnati Art Museum.

opposite below: CROPSEY: Eagle Cliff. 1851. Oil, 35 x 53″. Private collection.

Frederick E. CHURCH: Cotopaxi, Ecuador. 1862. Oil, 48 x 85″. New York Public Library, Lenox Collection.

BIERSTADT: Snow Scene with Buffaloes. 1860s? Oil, 18 x 24". Private collection.

KENSETT: Seashore. 1860. Oil, 18 x 30″. New York Public Library, Stuart Collection.

William H. BEARD: The Balloon. 1882. Oil, 48 x 33½″. Collection Victor D. Spark.

William PAGE: Portrait of Mrs. Page. c. 1860.
Oil, 60¼ x 36¼". Detroit Institute of Arts.

VEDDER: The Lair of the Sea Serpent. 1864.
Oil, 21⅛ x 36⅛". Museum of Fine Arts, Boston.

Martin J. HEADE: Storm Approaching Larchmont Bay. 1868. Oil, 32⅛ x 54⅜″. Collection Ernest Rosenfeld.

JOHNSON: Girl Picking Water Lilies. 1865. Oil, 18½ x 15¼″. Collection Mr. and Mrs. I. M. Cohen.

JOHNSON: *Study for* The Wounded Drummer Boy. c. 1870?. Oil, 26¼ x 21½″. Fine Arts Society of San Diego.

HUNT: The Bathers. 1877. Oil, 24 x 16″. Worcester Art Museum.

HUNT: The Ball Players. Oil, 16 x 24″. Detroit Institute of Arts.

LA FARGE: Portrait of the Artist. 1859. Oil, 16 x 11½″. Metropolitan Museum of Art.

WHISTLER: Nocturne in Blue and Silver: The Lagoon, Venice. c. 1880. Oil, 20⅛ x 25⅞″. Museum of Fine Arts, Boston.

EAKINS: Elizabeth at the Piano. 1875. Oil, 72 x 48″. Addison Gallery of American Art, Andover.

INNESS: The Monk. 1873. Oil, 38½ x 64½″. Collection Stephen C. Clark.

INNESS: The Approaching Storm. c. 1880. Oil, 27½ x 42″. Addison Gallery of American Art.

T. MORAN.

BLAKELOCK: Moonlight. 1889. Oil, 27¼ x 32¼". Brooklyn Museum.

opposite above: MORAN: Cliffs of the Upper Colorado River, Wyoming Territory. 1882. Oil, 15⅝ x 23½". National Collection of Fine Arts, Washington.

opposite below: REMINGTON: Fired On. Oil, 26⅜ x 39¼". National Collection of Fine Arts, Washington.

HOMER: The Gulf Stream. 1899. Oil, 30½ x 50¼″. Metropolitan Museum of Art.

opposite above: HOMER: The Fox Hunt. 1893. Oil, 38 x 68″. Pennsylvania Academy of the Fine Arts. *Not in the exhibition.*

opposite below: HOMER: Summer Night. 1890. Oil, 30¼ x 40⅛″. Jeu de Paume Museum, Paris. *Not in the exhibition.*

LA FARGE: The Wolf Charmer. 1907. Oil, 80½ x 62½″. Washington University, St. Louis.

NEWMAN: The Fortune Teller. Oil, 10 x 14″. Metropolitan Museum of Art.

DEWING: The Recitation. 1891. Oil, 30 x 55″. Detroit Institute of Arts.

SARGENT: Robert Louis Stevenson. 1885. Oil, 20¼ x 24¼″. Collection Mrs. Payne Whitney.

RYDER: Macbeth and the Witches. 1890–1908. Oil, 28½ x 36″. Phillips Memorial Gallery, Washington.

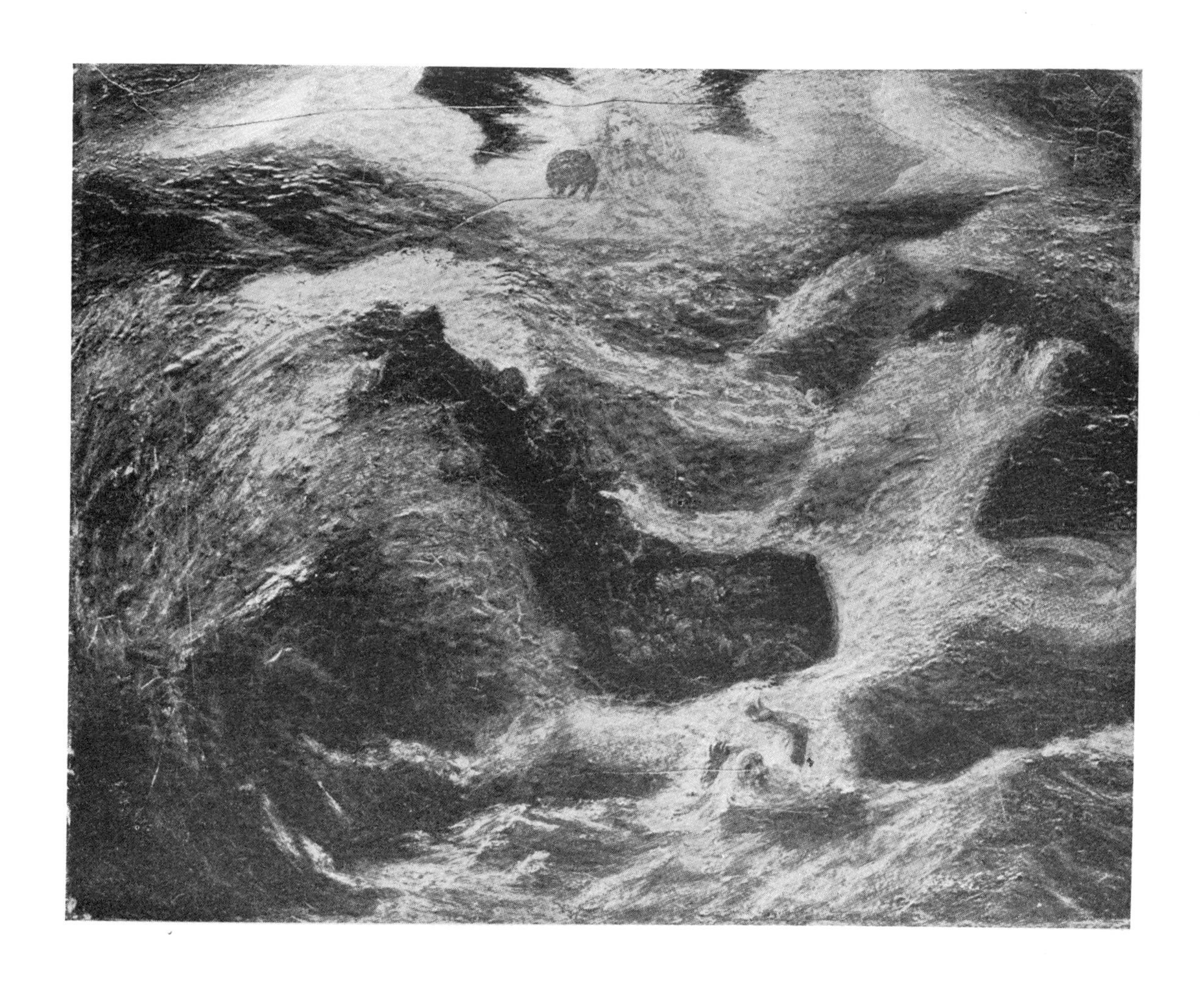

RYDER: Jonah. Oil, $27\frac{1}{8}$ x $34\frac{3}{8}$". National Collection of Fine Arts, Washington. *Not in the exhibition.*

RYDER: Moonlight—Marine. Oil, 11⅜ x 12″. Metropolitan Museum of Art.

RYDER: Dead Bird. 1890–1900. Oil, 4¼ x 9⅞″. Phillips Memorial Gallery.

Arthur B. DAVIES: Along the Erie Canal. 1890. Oil, 18¼ x 40″. Phillips Memorial Gallery.

DAVIES: Dream. Before 1909. Oil, 18 x 30″. Metropolitan Museum of Art.

EILSHEMIUS: Don Quixote. 1895. Oil, 20 x 30″. Kleemann Galleries.

EILSHEMIUS: Jealousy. 1915. Oil, 19½ x 25″. Valentine Gallery.

George BELLOWS: The Picnic. 1924. Oil, 30 x 44″. Lewisohn Collection.

BELLOWS: A Knock-out. 1921. Lithograph, 15¼ x 21¾″. Albert H. Wiggin Collection, Boston Public Library.

Edward HOPPER: Cape Cod Evening. 1939. Oil, 30 x 40″. Frank K. M. Rehn Gallery.

opposite above: John SLOAN: The City from Greenwich Village. 1922. Oil, 26 x 34″. Kraushaar Galleries.

opposite below: Rockwell KENT: Toilers of the Sea. 1907. Oil, 37½ x 44″. Lewisohn Collection.

Georgia O'KEEFFE: Black Cross, New Mexico. 1929. Oil, 39 x 30". Art Institute of Chicago.

John MARIN: Sunset, Casco Bay. 1919. Watercolor, 16 x 19½″. Collection Georgia O'Keeffe.

Marsden HARTLEY: Evening Storm, Schoodic, Maine. 1942. Oil, 30 x 40″. Museum of Modern Art.

opposite above: Max WEBER: Chassidic Dance. 1940. Oil, 32 x 40″. Collection Mr. and Mrs. Milton Lowenthal.

opposite below: WEBER: Winter Twilight. 1940. Oil, 30 x 40″. Collection Mr. and Mrs. Buell Hammett.

C. S. PRICE: Fisherman. 1941. Oil, 34 x 42″. Detroit Institute of Arts.

opposite above: Benjamin KOPMAN: A Lynching. 1930. Oil, 29 x 47″. Collection Mr. and Mrs. Bernard Reis.

opposite below: William GROPPER: The Defenders. 1941. Oil, 20 x 24″. A.C.A. Gallery.

Karl ZERBE: Terror. 1943. Encaustic, 29 x 36½". Downtown Gallery.

Theodore C. POLOS: Green Landscape. 1940. Oil, 16¼ x 20". Owned by the artist.

George GROSZ: No Let-up. 1940. Oil, 29 x 21″. Collection Mr. and Mrs. Frederick B. Adams, Jr.

Joseph DE MARTINI: Self-portrait. 1943. Oil, 48 x 30″. Phillips Memorial Gallery.

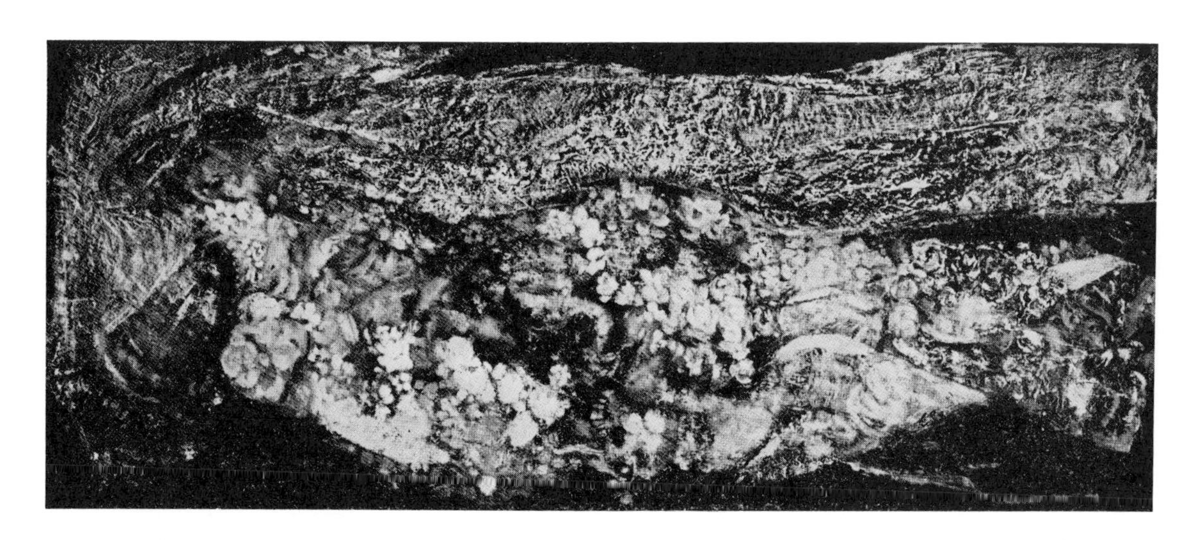

Hyman BLOOM: The Bride. 1941. Oil, 20⅛ x 49⅞″. Museum of Modern Art.

Donald FORBES: Millstone. c. 1936. Oil, 26¼ x 36″. WPA Art Program.

Lyonel FEININGER: Steamer Odin. 1927. Oil, 26½ x 39½″. Buchholz Gallery.

FEININGER: The Bird Cloud. 1926. Oil, 17⅝ x 28⅛″. Collection J. B. Neumann.

DEMUTH: Two illustrations for *The Turn of the Screw* by Henry James. 1918. Watercolor, 8 x 10⅜". Collection Frank C. Osborn.

Charles BURCHFIELD: House of Mystery. 1924. Tempera with oil glaze, 29½ x 23½″. Art Institute of Chicago.

opposite: BURCHFIELD: Church Bells Ringing—Rainy Winter Night. 1917. Watercolor, 30 x 19″. Collection Mrs. Louise M. Dunn.

BURCHFIELD: The First Hepaticas. 1918. Watercolor, 21½ x 27½″. Museum of Modern Art.

Morris KANTOR: Haunted House. 1930. Oil, 37 x 33¼". Art Institute of Chicago.

Hobson PITTMAN: Old Friends. c. 1940. Oil, 30⅛ x 40¼″. Collection Philip L. Goodwin.

Aaron BOHROD: Tourist House. 1941. Oil, 21 x 28½. Associated American Artists.

Philip EVERGOOD: My Forebears Were Pioneers. 1938-39. Oil, 48¾ x 35½″. Collection Lt. and Mrs. Bruce Ryan.

Henry MATTSON: Stars and Sea. 1941. Oil, 36 x 42″. Frank K. M. Rehn Gallery.

opposite above: MATTSON: Jungle Play. 1941. Oil, 26 x 40″. Frank K. M. Rehn Gallery.

opposite below: Paul MOMMER: At Night. 1940. Oil, 30 x 40″. Owned by the artist.

Matthew BARNES: High Peak. 1936. Oil, 36½ x 42¼″. Owned by the artist.

opposite above: Elliot ORR: Desecration. 1941. 24 x 30″. Collection Lt. and Mrs. Alastair Bradley-Martin.

opposite below: John C. PELLEW: East River Nocturne, No. 2. 1941. Oil, 28¼ x 36¼″. Contemporary Arts.

Bernard KARFIOL: Boy. 1924. Oil, 36 x 27″. Phillips Memorial Gallery.

Julian LEVI: Buoys. 1939. Oil, 18 x 22″. Collection John L. Sexton.

John CARROLL: Rate de Ballet. 1941. Oil, 60 x 30″. Honolulu Academy of Arts.

Alexander BROOK: The Tragic Muse. 1933. Oil, 40 x 24″. Newark Museum.

Alexander BROOK: Pasture at Elk. 1939. Oil, 20 x 28″. Wadsworth Atheneum, Hartford.

Eugene LUDINS: Interlude. 1940. Oil, 36½ x 48¾″. Associated American Artists.

opposite above: Arnold BLANCH: Suwannee River. 1940. Oil, 30 x 48″. Associated American Artists

opposite below: Roff BEMAN: Brummitt's Cornfield. 1939. Oil, 24¼ x 36¼″. WPA Art Program.

William C. PALMER: Spring Landscape with Ruins. 1938. Tempera and oil, 24 x 30″. Midtown Galleries.

Robert ARCHER: Approaching Storm. c. 1938. Oil, 24¼ x 30¼″. WPA Art Program.

John Steuart CURRY: Hogs Killing a Rattlesnake. 1932. Oil, 30 x 38″. Associated American Artists.

Thomas BENTON: Moonlight on the Osage. 1938. Tempera, 14 x 17¼″. Collection Boetius H. Sullivan, Jr.

Franklin C. WATKINS: Suicide in Costume. 1931. Oil, 36¼ x 44¼″. Philadelphia Museum of Art.

WATKINS: Soliloquy. 1932. Oil, 25 x 30″. Whitney Museum of American Art.

Elizabeth SPARHAWK-JONES: Lady Godiva. 1941. Watercolor, 20 x 24″. Collection Mrs. Otto L. Spaeth.

Rico LEBRUN: Migration to Nowhere. 1941. Gouache, 30 x 48″. Owned by the artist.

Jon CORBINO: Stampeding Bulls. 1937. Oil, 28 x 41⅞″. Toledo Museum of Art.

Edwin DICKINSON: Figures and Still Life. 1933–37. Oil, 97 x 77¾″. Passedoit Gallery.

John ATHERTON: Foggy Day. 1941. Oil, 26⅛ x 36⅛″. Julien Levy Gallery.

Walter STUEMPFIG: Dalliance at Cape May. 1943. Oil, 30 x 36″. Durlacher Brothers.

above: Raymond BREININ: The Cloak. 1943. Oil, 32 x 50″. Downtown Gallery.
below left: Richard BLOW: The Painter. 1938. Oil, 28 x 32″. Metropolitan Museum of Art.
below right: Arthur OSVER: Melancholy of a Rooftop. 1942. Oil, 48 x 24″. Museum of Modern Art.

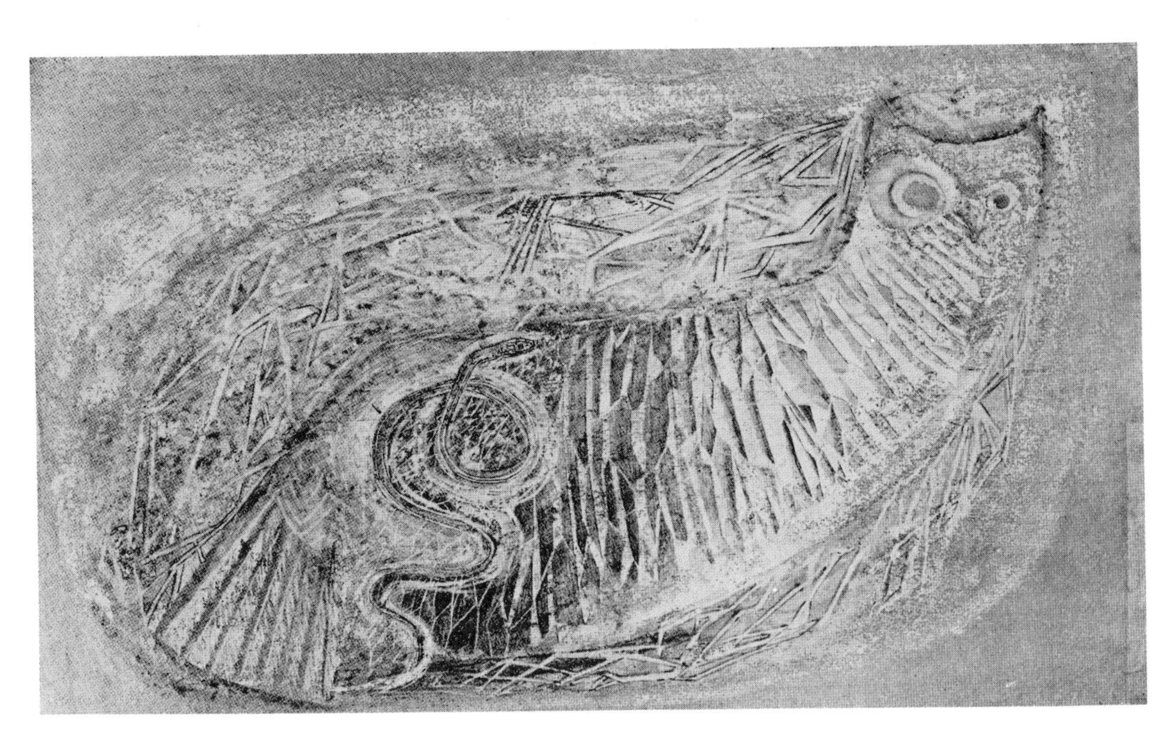

Morris GRAVES: Owl of the Inner Eye. 1941. Gouache, 20¾ x 36⅝″. Museum of Modern Art.

William FETT: The Dangerous Night. 1943. Watercolor, 17¼ x 26¾″. Smith College Museum of Art.

Loren MacIVER: The Violet Hour. 1943. Oil, $90\frac{1}{2} \times 57\frac{3}{4}''$. Pierre Matisse Gallery.

Darrel AUSTIN: The Black Beast. 1941. Oil, 24 x 30″. Smith College Museum of Art.

Julia THECLA: This. 1936. Pastel and watercolor, 19¼ x 14″. Collection David Porter.

Biographies of the Artists and Catalog of the Exhibition

An asterisk (*) indicates that the work is illustrated. Works not illustrated here bear a reference if reproduced in another of the Museum's publications. Unless otherwise stated, all paintings are oil on canvas. *Dimensions are in inches and height precedes width.*

ALLSTON, Washington. 1779-1843. Born on plantation, Waccamaw region, S. C.; grew up in Newport, R. I. Harvard 1800, class poet. Returned to Charleston; 1801 to England with Malbone; studied Royal Academy under Benjamin West. 1804 to Paris with Vanderlyn to study art collected by Napoleon; then 4 years in Rome, where he knew Coleridge, Washington Irving, Thorwaldson. 1809 returned to America; 1811 to England with Morse. Successful professional and social career in England 1811-17. 1818 returned to America; studio in Boston, later in Cambridgeport. Essayist, poet, critic, teacher, a brilliant leader in Boston's cultural life for 25 years. Died Cambridgeport.

*1 The Deluge. 1804. 48 x 65¾". Lent by Metropolitan Museum of Art. *Ill. p.53.*

2 Rising of a Thunderstorm at Sea. 1804. 38½ x 51". Lent by Museum of Fine Arts, Boston.

*3 Diana and Her Nymphs in the Chase (Swiss Scenery). 1805. 66¼ x 97¾". Lent by Mrs. Algernon Coolidge. *Ill. p.52.*

4 Portrait of Samuel Taylor Coleridge (unfinished). 1806. 30 x 25". Lent by Henry Wadsworth Longfellow Dana.

ARCHER, Robert. Born 1905. Worked on WPA Art Project, New York.

*5 Approaching Storm. c. 1938. 24¼ x 30¼". WPA Art Program. *Ill. p.118.*

ATHERTON, John. Born Brainerd, Minn. 1900; State of Washington 1906-18. U. S. Navy 1918-19. Worked in mines, shipyards, at sign painting, etc. California School of Fine Arts, San Francisco 1922-25. Since 1926, successful advertising artist. To New York 1929. Lives Ridgefield, Conn.

*6 Foggy Day. 1941. 26⅛ x 36⅛". Lent by Julien Levy Gallery. *Ill. p.124.*

AUDUBON, John James. 1785-1851. Born Les Cayes, Santo Domingo, son of wealthy French naval officer. Brought up in France; studied drawing in David's studio. Childhood interest in ornithology. 1803 to father's estate in Pennsylvania. 1807, after unsuccessful business ventures, to Kentucky to open frontier store; neglected business for bird study which increasingly absorbed him; by 1810 had made 200 drawings. 1812-19 at Henderson, Ky.; bankrupt, began drawing portraits. 1819-20 position in Dr. Daniel Drake's natural history museum, Cincinnati; decided on unprecedented project: to portray all the birds of America, in full action and in natural habitat. 1820 down Mississippi by flatboat to New Orleans; painted portraits, tutored, while pursuing project. 1826 sailed from New Orleans to Liverpool to find publisher for drawings. Successful in London, Edinburgh, Paris; got subscribers; elected to learned and scientific societies. Publication of *The Birds of America* begun 1827 by Lizars of Edinburgh, completed by Havell of London 1838. Visit to America 1829; return to England 1830. Published *Ornithological Biography* 1831-39, to accompany *The Birds of America.* 1831 to America to continue and complete bird studies in Florida, Labrador, etc. 1839 began work on *Quadrupeds of America*, going west to North Dakota and Montana; publication begun 1845. Died New York.

7 White-headed Eagle. 1828. Aquatint colored by hand, 25¼ x 38¼". Lent by Old Print Shop.

*8 Barn Owl. 1833. Aquatint colored by hand, 33¾ x 22⅞". Lent by Weyhe Gallery. *Ill. p.59.*

9 Wood Ibis. 1834. Aquatint colored by hand, 34⅜ x 27⅞". Lent by Old Print Shop.

*10 Canada Lynx. 1845. Lithograph colored by hand, 21⅜ x 27⅛". Lent by Kennedy & Co. *Ill. p.59.*

AUSTIN, Darrel. Born Raymond, Wash. 1907. Grew up in Portland, Ore. Studied art Columbia University, Notre Dame and in Portland. Worked on Oregon WPA Art Project. Lives New York.

*11 The Black Beast. 1941. 24 x 30". Lent by Smith College Museum of Art. *Ill. p.128.*

12 The Dark River. 1941. 20 x 24". Lent by Phillips Memorial Gallery.

13 The Black Bullock. 1942. 20 x 24". Lent by Perls Galleries.

BARNES, Matthew. Born Scotland 1880. To U. S. 1904; New York until 1906; then settled San Francisco. Self-taught. Worked on California WPA Art Project.

14 Night Scene. 1932. 36⅜ x 42¼".

*15 High Peak. 1936. 36½ x 42¼". *Ill. p.111.*

16 Ghost Homes. 1938. 20 x 24″.
Nos. 14-16, lent by the artist.

BEARD, William Holbrook. 1825-1900. Born Painesville, Ohio. Itinerant portrait painter; 1850 worked in Buffalo, N. Y. Studied and painted in Rome, Switzerland, Düsseldorf. Settled in New York 1860. Popular in his day for paintings of animals satirizing human foibles. Died New York.

17 The Witches' Sabbath. 1876. 38¼ x 58⅜″. Lent by Robert C. Vose Galleries.

*18 The Balloon. 1882. 48 x 33½″. Lent by Victor D. Spark. *Ill. p.68.*

BELLOWS, George Wesley. 1882-1925. Born Columbus, Ohio. Ohio State University; newspaper cartoonist in spare time. Studied with H. G. Maratta, Chicago; 1904 New York with Henri and Hayes Miller. Taught Art Students' League and National Academy (1913). Brilliant younger member of Henri's group although did not exhibit with "The Eight." Died New York.

19 Dance in a Madhouse. 1917. Lithograph, 18¼ x 24½″. Lent by H. V. Allison & Co.

*20 A Knock-out. 1921. Lithograph, 15¼ x 21¾″. Lent by Albert H. Wiggin Collection, Boston Public Library. *Ill. p.87.*

*21 The Picnic. 1924. 30 x 44″. Lent by Lewisohn Collection. *Ill. p.87.*

BEMAN, Roff. 1891-1940. Born Chicago. Studied in Paris; with Sloan and Emil Armin. Worked on Illinois WPA Art Project. Lived in Chicago.

*22 Brummitt's Cornfield. 1939. 24¼ x 36¼″. WPA Art Program. *Ill. p.116.*

BENTON, Thomas Hart. Born Neosho, Mo. 1889. At 17 newspaper cartoonist, studying Art Institute of Chicago. 1908 to Paris for 5 years. U. S. Navy, World War. After 1925 identified with American regionalist movement. Murals, New School for Social Research (1930) were among first non-academic American mural paintings; other murals, Whitney Museum, N. Y., Indianapolis, Jefferson City, Mo. Taught Art Students' League, New School for Social Research, Kansas City Art Institute. 1943 artist-correspondent on U. S. Navy project. Lives Kansas City.

*23 Moonlight on the Osage. 1938. Tempera on gesso, 14 x 17¼″. Lent by Pfc. Boetius H. Sullivan, Jr. *Ill. p.119.*

BIERSTADT, Albert. 1830-1902. Born Solingen, Germany. To America at 2 years, grew up in New Bedford, Mass. 1853 to Düsseldorf to study 4 years; worked in Rome and Switzerland. Returned to U. S. 1857; 1858 joined expedition through unopened territories of West, followed by several later trips. Hugh canvases of Rockies and other Western scenery popular here and abroad in '60s and '70s; received medals from Czar of Russia, Sultan of Turkey and others. Died New York.

24 A Stream in the Rocky Mountains. c. 1860. 39⅛ x 30⅛. Lent by A. F. Mondschein.

*25 Snow Scene with Buffaloes. 1860s? Oil on millboard, 18 x 24″. Lent anonymously. *Ill. p.67.*

BINGHAM, George Caleb. 1811-79. Born Augusta Co., Va.; with family to Missouri 1819. c. 1827 cabinet maker's apprentice; studied law and theology; first painting instruction supposedly from Chester Harding. c. 1830 began to paint portraits of neighbors. c. 1835 to St. Louis; c. 1837 to study at Pennsylvania Academy, Philadelphia. 1840-44 painted portraits, Washington, D. C.; to Missouri 1844. First genre and landscape paintings 1845. Visit to New York 1849; in Philadelphia 1853-54. To Europe 1856; in Düsseldorf until 1859; returned to Missouri. In Union Army 1861. Active in state and local politics throughout life; professor of art, University of Missouri 1877. Died Kansas City.

*26 Fur Traders Descending the Missouri. c. 1845. 29¼ x 36¼″. Lent by Metropolitan Museum of Art. *Ill. p.61.*

*27 Daniel Boone Escorting a Band of Pioneers into the Western Country. c. 1851. 37 x 50″. Lent by Washington University, St. Louis, through City Art Museum, St. Louis. *Ill.p.61.*

BLAKELOCK, Ralph Albert. 1847-1919. Born New York; graduated College of the City of N. Y. 1867; medical education but gave this up for music and painting. Could not afford instruction or European travel, worked alone, ignored by art circles and public. Worked his way through the West, inspired by scenery and Indian life. Returned to New York, painted under increasing financial and family difficulties. At 52 mental breakdown, 18 years in asylum. Never profited from increasing popularity and value of his paintings. Died in Adirondacks.

*28 Moonlight. 1889. 27¼ x 32¼″. Lent by Brooklyn Museum. *Ill. p.77.*

BLANCH, Arnold. Born Mantorville, Minn. 1896. Studied Minneapolis School of Fine Arts, Art Students' League. U. S. Army, World War, drawing maps for Intelligence Corps; after War 2 years in France and Italy. Guggenheim fellowship 1933; to Southern France. Taught California School of Fine Arts, Art Students' League, Colorado Springs Fine Arts Center. Section of Fine Arts murals, Norwalk, Conn., Fredonia, N. Y., Columbus, Wis.; worked on WPA Art Project, New York. Lives Woodstock, N. Y.

*29 Suwannee River. 1940. 30 x 48". Lent by Associated American Artists. *Ill. p.116.*

BLOOM, Hyman. Born Latvia 1913. To U. S. 1920, living ever since in Boston. Studied under Harold Zimmerman and Denman Ross, Boston. Worked on Massachusetts WPA Art Project.

30 Skeleton. c. 1936. 12 x 68". Lent by Nat Sharfman.

*31 The Bride. 1941. 20⅛ x 49⅞". Museum of Modern Art, Purchase Fund. *Ill. p.99.*

BLOW, Richard. Born La Salle, Ill. 1904. Studied National Academy, Art Students' League, Art Institute of Chicago. Before the war lived Florence, Italy and New York. Now in U. S. Army.

*32 The Painter. 1938. Oil on fibre board, 28 x 32". Lent by Metropolitan Museum of Art. *Ill. p.125.*

BOHROD, Aaron. Born Chicago 1907. Studied Art Institute of Chicago; 1929 to New York, Art Students' League 2 years with Boardman Robinson, Sloan, Hayes Miller. Guggenheim fellowship 1936, renewal 1937. Worked on Illinois WPA Art Project. Section of Fine Arts murals, Clinton, Galesburg and Vandalia, Ill. 1942 artist-in-residence, Southern Illinois Normal University. 1943 to South Pacific as artist-correspondent. Lives Chicago.

*33 Tourist House. 1941. Oil on composition board, 21 x 28½". Lent by Associated American Artists. *Ill. p.106.*

BREININ, Raymond. Born Vitebsk, Russia 1910. To U. S. 1923. Studied Art Institute of Chicago, Chicago Academy of Art. Worked on Illinois WPA Art Project; Section of Fine Arts murals, Wilmette, Ill. Artist-in-residence, Southern Illinois Normal University, Carbondale.

*34 The Cloak. 1943. 32 x 50". Lent by Downtown Gallery. *Ill. p.125.*

BROOK, Alexander. Born Brooklyn 1898, of Russian parentage. Studied Pratt Institute, Brooklyn; Art Students' League. 1924-27 assistant director, Whitney Studio Club. Guggenheim fellowship 1931. Section of Fine Arts mural, Post Office Department, Washington. 1943 to Panama and Caribbean as artist-correspondent. Lives in New York.

*35 The Tragic Muse. 1933. 40 x 24". Lent by Newark Museum. *Ill. p.115.*

*36 Pasture at Elk. 1939. 20 x 28". Lent by Wadsworth Atheneum. *Ill. p.115.*

BROWN, Eliphalet, Jr., publisher, New York.

37 U. S. Steam Frigate Mississippi in a Typhoon. 1857. Lithograph colored by hand, 16 x 20¾". Lent by Old Print Shop.

BURCHFIELD, Charles. Born Ashtabula Harbor, Ohio 1893. 1898-1921 lived in Salem, Ohio. 1911-16 Cleveland School of Art. Until 1921 worked as costs accountant in automobile parts factory. Army training camp 1918. 1921-28 in Buffalo, N. Y. as wallpaper designer; 1928 resigned job to devote full time to painting. Lives Gardenville, N. Y.

38 Garden of Memories. 1917. Crayon and watercolor, 25¾ x 22½". Museum of Modern Art, gift of Mrs. John D. Rockefeller, Jr. (by exchange). Ill. *Burchfield*, no. 25.

*39 Church Bells Ringing—Rainy Winter Night. 1917. Watercolor, 30 x 19". Lent by Mrs. Louise M. Dunn. *Ill. p.103.*

40 The Night Wind. 1918. Watercolor, 21¼ x 21¾". Lent by A. Conger Goodyear. *Ill. color portfolio, no. 18.*

*41 The First Hepaticas. 1918. Watercolor, 21½ x 27½". Museum of Modern Art, gift of Mrs. John D. Rockefeller, Jr. *Ill. p.102.*

*42 House of Mystery. 1924. Tempera with oil glaze on board, 29½ x 23½". Lent by Art Institute of Chicago. *Ill. p.102.*

CARROLL, John. Born Kansas City, Kan. 1892. Studied Mark Hopkins Institute, San Francisco, 1903-06; University of California 1911; and with Frank Duveneck 1913-15. U. S. Navy, World War. To Paris on Guggenheim fellowship 1926. Taught Art Students' League, Society of Arts and Crafts, Detroit. Section of Fine Arts mural, Clemson, S. C. Lives East Chatham, N. Y.

*43 Rate de Ballet. 1941. 60 x 30". Lent by Honolulu Academy of Arts. *Ill. p.114.*

CATLIN, George. 1796-1872. Born Wyoming Valley, Pa. 1817-18 studied law, practised 2 or 3 years; then self-taught portrait painter; 1824-30 painted in Washington, Albany, Richmond. 1829 saw group of Western

Indians in Philadelphia on way to Washington; inspired to devote talents to recording Indian life. 1832 for about 8 years traveled among 48 tribes making 310 oil portraits and 200 oils recording ceremonies, hunting, villages, etc. 1841 published *Illustrations of the Manners, Customs, and Condition of the North American Indians.* 1837-52 "Indian Gallery" with accompanying troupe of Indians toured U. S., England, France. 1846 collection offered to Smithsonian Institution; accepted 1879. Traveled and painted in South and Central America 1852-57; in Europe 1858-70. Died Jersey City, N. J.

*44 "Ha-wón-je-tah, the One Horn; first chief of the tribe; Mee-ne-cow-e-gee band. Upper Missouri [Sioux (Dah-co-ta)]; hair tied on his head in form of a turban, and filled with glue and red earth, or vermilion." c. 1832. 27⅛ x 23″. *Ill. p.60.*

45 "View on Upper Missouri—Back view of the Mandan Village, showing their mode of depositing their dead, on scaffolds, enveloped in skins, and of preserving and feeding the skulls; 1800 miles above St. Louis. Women feeding the skulls of their relatives with dishes of meat." c. 1832. 11⅛ x 14⅜″.

46 "Buffalo Hunt under the wolf-skin mask." c. 1832. 19 x 26½″.
Nos. 44-46, lent by United States National Museum, Smithsonian Institution.

47 Flamingo Shooting in South America. 1857. 19 x 26½″. Lent by Rochester Memorial Art Gallery.

CHAMBERS, T. Active 1820-40. Painted Hudson River region, Natural Bridge, Washington's tomb, Niagara Falls, Franconia Notch, New York and Boston Harbors.

48 Niagara Falls. c. 1820-40. 21¼ x 29½″. Lent by Wadsworth Atheneum, Hartford.

CHURCH, Frederick Edwin. 1826-1900. Born Hartford, Conn. Pupil of Thomas Cole at Catskill, N. Y. First painted Catskills, then 1853 and 1857 to South America to paint the Andes; later to Labrador to paint icebergs. 1866 to Jamaica; 1868 first visit to Europe and Near East. Extremely successful, U. S. and Europe. Died New York.

*49 Cotopaxi, Ecuador. 1862. 48 x 85″. Lent by New York Public Library, Lenox Collection. *Ill. p.66.*

CODMAN, Charles. 1800-42. Painted clock faces, signs and fire buckets until about 1828. Became successful landscape painter. Exhibited at Boston Atheneum 1828-34. Lived Portland, Me.

50 The Pirates' Cove. c. 1830. 23¼ x 31″. Lent by Old Print Shop.

COLE, Thomas. 1801-48. Born Bolton-le-Moors, Lancashire, England. As child worked on engravings for calico in a print works. At 19 to U. S. with family, living Philadelphia, then Steubenville, Ohio, where he worked with father in wallpaper factory. Taught himself to paint; itinerant portrait painter. 2 winters in Philadelphia in extreme poverty; then 1825 to New York where his landscape paintings attracted enthusiasm of Trumbull, Durand, Dunlap. Inspired by Hudson River and Catskill scenery and romantic literature dealing with the region; established studio at Catskill, N. Y. 1829 to England, France, Italy until 1832. Again to Europe 1841-42. Pioneer painter of landscape in this country. Died Catskill, N. Y.

51 Scene from Cooper's *The Last of the Mohicans.* 1827. 25½ x 35″. Lent by Wadsworth Atheneum.

52 Mt. Chocorua, New Hampshire. 1827. Oil on wood, 23 x 32″. Lent anonymously.

*53 The Expulsion from Eden. 1828. 39 x 53¾″. Lent anonymously, through Museum of Fine Arts, Boston. *Ill. p.54.*

*54 The Oxbow (Connecticut River near Northampton). 1836. 51½ x 76″. Lent by Metropolitan Museum of Art. *Ill. p.55.*

55 The Vision. c. 1846? Oil on wood, 12 x 18″. Lent by Brooklyn Museum.

COPLEY, John Singleton. 1737 or 1738-1815. Born Boston, of Irish parentage. Encouraged by stepfather, Peter Pelham, the engraver, started career as portrait painter. Became our most eminent Colonial painter; successful career in New England and other colonies. To Europe 1774, visiting Italy and settling in London the following year; never returned to America. Became one of London's leading painters of portraits, historical and religious canvases. Died London.

56 Watson and the Shark. Ink, 19 x 23½″. Lent by Museum of Historic Art, Princeton University.

*57 Watson and the Shark. 1778. 72⅛ x 90¼″. Lent by Museum of Fine Arts, Boston. *Ill. p.49.*

CORBINO, Jon. Born Vittoria, Sicily 1905. To New York 1913. Studied art Ethical Culture School, N. Y.; Art Students' League, Pennsylvania Academy. Originally a sculptor, then painter. Guggenheim fellowships 1936 and 1937. Section of Fine Arts mural, Long Beach, N. Y.; worked on WPA Art Project. Teaches summer school, Rockport, Mass. Lives Scarsdale, N. Y.

*58 Stampeding Bulls. 1937. 28 x 41⅞″. Lent by Toledo Museum of Art. *Ill. p.122.*

COWLES, Russell. Born Algona, Iowa 1887. Studied National Academy, Art Students' League; American Academy in Rome fellowship 1915-17. U.S. Naval Intelligence, Italy, 1917-20. Traveled Europe and Far East; worked 10 years in New Mexico. Lives New York.

59 Old World. 1943. 43½ x 30½". Lent by Kraushaar Galleries.

CROPSEY, Jasper Francis. 1823-1900. Born Rossville, Staten Island, N. Y. Worked in architect's office 5 years. Turned to landscape painting, studied National Academy. 1847 to Europe, 3 years in Italy; 1857-63 studio in London. In brief return to architecture, designed "El" stations in N. Y. C. Painted chiefly Hudson River scenery. Died Hastings-on-Hudson, N. Y.

*60 Eagle Cliff. 1851. 35 x 53". Lent anonymously, through Museum of Fine Arts, Boston, *Ill. p.65.*

CURRIER and IVES. Between 1835 and 1907 Nathaniel Currier and the succeeding firm of Currier & Ives, a partnership formed in 1857, published some 6,700 different lithographs.

*61 The Life of a Hunter. A Tight Fix. 1861. Colored lithograph, after painting by Arthur F. Tait, 18¾ x 27". *Ill. p.62.*

62 Life on the Prairie—The Trapper's Defense. "Fire Fight Fire." 1862. Colored lithograph, after painting by Arthur F. Tait, 18½ x 27⅛."

*63 The Lightning Express Trains. Leaving the Junction. 1863. Colored lithograph by Fanny F. Palmer, 17⅞ x 27⅞". *Ill. p.62.*

64 The Champions of the Mississippi. A Race for the Buckhorns. 1866. Colored lithograph by Fanny F. Palmer, 18¼ x 27¾". Ill. *Trois Siècles d'Art aux Etats-Unis*, pl. 10.

65 The Great Fire at Chicago, Oct. 8, 1871. Colored lithograph, 16⅞ x 24½".
Nos. 61-65, lent by Harry T. Peters.

CURRY, John Steuart. Born Dunavant, Kan. 1897; grew up on father's farm. 1916 Kansas City Art Institute; Chicago Art Institute; Art Students' League; Russian Academy, Paris. 1932 traveled several months with Ringling Brothers Circus. Section of Fine Arts murals, Departments of Justice and Interior, Washington. Since 1936 artist-in-residence, University of Wisconsin.

*66 Hogs Killing a Rattlesnake. 1932. 30 x 38". Lent by Associated American Artists. *Ill. p.119.*

DAVIES, Arthur Bowen. 1862-1928. Born Utica, N. Y. At 18 to Mexico as draftsman for engineering expedition. Studied Academy of Design, Chicago; Art Institute of Chicago, and in New York. Magazine illustrator. To Italy 1893; influenced by Giorgione, El Greco, Blake, Cubism, Persian miniatures, Greek vase painting. 1908 exhibited with "The Eight", New York; president and moving spirit of Association of American Painters and Sculptors, which organized Armory Show, New York, 1913. Traveled widely; tapestries, prints, sculpture, as well as painting. Died near Florence, Italy.

*67 Along the Erie Canal. 1890. 18¼ x 40". Lent by Phillips Memorial Gallery. *Ill. p. 85.*

*68 Dream. Before 1909. 18 x 30". Lent by Metropolitan Museum of Art. *Ill. p.85.*

De MARTINI, Joseph. Born Mobile, Ala. 1896. Studied National Academy. Worked on WPA Art Project, New York. Lives New York.

69 Moonlit Cove. 1941. 26 x 32". Lent by George L. Shaskan.

*70 Self-portrait. 1943. 48 x 30". Lent by Phillips Memorial Gallery. *Ill. p.98.*

DEMUTH, Charles. 1883-1935. Born Lancaster, Pa. Studied Pennsylvania Academy under Chase and Anshutz; 1904 to Paris for 2 years. 1912 again to Paris, Colarossi Academy. 1914 return to U. S. Outstanding watercolorist; vaudeville subjects, architecture, still life, illustrations for Henry James, Zola, Poe, Balzac. Lived in Lancaster with frequent trips to New York. Died Lancaster.

Five illustrations for *The Turn of the Screw* by Henry James. 1918. Watercolor, each 8 x 10⅜":

71 "She had picked up a small flat piece of wood . . ." Ill. *Modern Painters and Sculptors as Illustrators*, p.91.

*72 "Did I steal?" *Ill. p.101.*

73 "I can see—the way—his hand—passed from one crenelation to the next."

*74 "Mrs. Grose watched them with positive placidity . . ." *Ill. p.101.*
Nos. 71-74, lent by Frank C. Osborn.

75 "At a House in Harley Street." 8 x 11". Museum of Modern Art, gift of Mrs. John D. Rockefeller, Jr.

DEWING, Thomas Wilmer. 1851-1938. Born Boston. Pupil of Lefebvre and Boulanger, Paris, 1876-79. Settled in New York. With Twachtman, Weir, Tarbell and others, 1898, formed "Ten American Painters," group which opposed academic tradition and favored individual experiment. Painted very little after 1920. Freer Gallery, Washington, set aside room for his paintings, pastels and silverpoints. Died New York.

*76 The Recitation. 1891. 30 x 55". Lent by Detroit Institute of Arts. *Ill. p.81.*

DICKINSON, Edwin W. Born Seneca Falls, N. Y. 1891. Studied with Chase and Charles Hawthorne. To France 1937. Taught 1939 Art Institute of Buffalo, Art Students' League. Worked on Massachusetts WPA Art Project. Lived at Provincetown; now lives Wellfleet, Mass.

*77 Figures and Still Life. 1933-37. 97 x 77¾". Lent by Passedoit Gallery. *Ill. p.123.*

78 Portrait of a Man. 1941. 20 x 23". Lent by Passedoit Gallery.

DOUGHTY, Thomas. 1793-1856. Born Philadelphia. Abandoned successful career as leather merchant to paint. Self-taught, one of first Americans to paint landscapes exclusively; forerunner of Cole in founding native landscape school. Scenes painted near Philadelphia and New York popular in Paris, London and U. S., but met with little financial success. Died New York.

79 In Nature's Wonderland. 1835. 24¼ x 30". Lent by Detroit Institute of Arts.

DUNCANSON, Robert S. 1821-71. Negro, born Cincinnati. Spent part of boyhood in Canada, returning to Cincinnati where his talent attracted attention about 1840. Sent to study in Scotland by Anti-Slavery League. Upon return became respected member of Cincinnati group of artists; numerous portrait and mural commissions from prominent families. Returned to Europe, exhibited allegorical and historical canvases with considerable success in Glasgow, Edinburgh and London. Revisited Cincinnati late '60s, painted Western scene under influence of James H. Beard and Duveneck.

*80 Blue Hole, Flood Waters, Little Miami River. 1851. 29¼ x 42¼". Lent by Cincinnati Art Museum. *Ill. p.65.*

DURAND, Asher Brown. 1796-1886. Born Jefferson Village, N. J. 1812 apprenticed 5 years to engraver, Peter Maverick. 1820-23 engraved Trumbull's *Declaration of Independence*, which gained him prominence. About 1835 gave up successful career as commercial engraver of tickets, banknotes, etc.; turned to portrait painting, practising in Washington. 1840 to Europe, copying old masters in London and Italy. Upon return, 1841, devoted himself to landscape painting, working directly outdoors (unusual at the time). A founder of National Academy in 1826; succeeded Morse as its president, 1845-61. Died Jefferson Village, N. J.

*81 Kindred Spirits [Thomas Cole and William Cullen Bryant]. 1849. 45 x 36". Lent by New York Public Library. *Ill. p.57.*

EAKINS, Thomas. 1844-1916. Born Philadelphia. Studied Pennsylvania Academy; physician's course in anatomy, Jefferson Medical College. Paris 1866-69, École des Beaux-Arts under Gérôme, also with Bonnat and sculptor Dumont; traveled in Spain and other parts of Europe. Settled in Philadelphia 1870, painting, doing some sculpture, teaching at Pennsylvania Academy and Philadelphia Art Students' League. Series of rowing, sailing, hunting, baseball pictures 1871-75; prize fights 1888-89. Portraits, noted today for penetrating honesty, drew adverse criticism; greatly underestimated as an artist during his lifetime. Died Philadelphia.

*82 Elizabeth at the Piano. 1875. 72 x 48". Lent by Addison Gallery of American Art. *Ill. p.74.*

EILSHEMIUS, Louis Michel. 1864-1941. Born near Newark, N. J., of Dutch descent. Educated Geneva and Dresden. At 17 returned to America, studied bookkeeping, then agriculture at Cornell. Studied Art Students' League; 1886 under Bouguereau, Paris. Traveled Europe, Africa, South Seas, and U. S. for 20 years, occasionally returning to New York. Met Ryder 1908. Painting admired by Marcel Duchamp, 1917, at Independent show, New York, resulting in exhibitions, Société Anonyme 1920, 1924. A prolific painter until 1921, was little-known until after 1932, in spite of determined self-advertising. Died New York.

*83 Don Quixote. 1895. 20 x 30". Lent by Kleemann Galleries. *Ill. p.86.*

84 Afternoon Wind. 1899. 20 x 36". Museum of Modern Art, given anonymously. Ill. *Painting and Sculpture in the Museum of Modern Art*, p.37.

*85 Jealousy. 1915. Oil on board, 19½ x 25". Lent by Valentine Gallery. *Ill. p.86.*

EVERGOOD, Philip. Born New York 1901. Educated at Eton and Cambridge, England. Apprenticed to Havard Thomas, sculptor, Slade School, London 1921-23; Art Students' League, New York, 1923-24; Julian Academy, Paris, 1924; British Academy, Rome, 1925. 1940-41 artist-in-residence, Kalamazoo College, Mich. WPA mural, Richmond Hill, N. Y.; Section of Fine Arts mural, Jackson, Ga. Lives Woodside, Long Island.

*86 My Forebears Were Pioneers. 1938-39. 48¾ x 35½". Lent by Lt. and Mrs. Bruce Ryan. *Ill. p.107.*

FEININGER, Lyonel. Born New York 1871. Son of two musicians; studied violin. To Germany 1887. Abandoned musical career; art training Kunstgewerbeschule, Hamburg; Berlin Academy of Fine Arts. Widely known as illustrator and cartoonist for German and French papers, 1906-07 for *Chicago Tribune*. Turned to painting, studying in Paris 1907; influenced by Cubism. Exhibited with Marc, Kandinsky, Klee in Berlin 1913. Taught painting and graphic arts at Bauhaus, Weimar and Dessau 1919-34. Returned to U. S. 1936; 1937 taught at Mills College, Oakland, Calif. Lives New York.

*87 The Bird Cloud. 1926. 17⅝ x 28⅛". Lent by J. B. Neumann. *Ill. p.100.*

*88 Steamer Odin. 1927. 26½ x 39½". Lent by Buchholz Gallery. *Ill. p.100.*

93 Snake and Moon. 1938-39. Gouache and watercolor, 25½ x 30¼". Ill. *Americans 1942*, p.55.

*94 Blind Bird. 1940. Gouache, 30⅛ x 27". *Color frontispiece.*

95 Little Known Bird of the Inner Eye. 1941. Gouache, 21 x 36¾". Ill. *Americans 1942*, p.56.

*96 Owl of the Inner Eye. 1941. Gouache, 20¾ x 36⅝". *Ill. p.126.*

Nos. 93-96, Museum of Modern Art, Purchase Fund.

FETT, William. Born Ann Arbor, Mich. 1918. Studied Art Institute of Chicago 4 years, graduating 1941. To Mexico on traveling fellowship for 14 months. Lives Michoacán, Mexico.

*89 The Dangerous Night. 1943. Watercolor, 17¼ x 26¾". Lent by Smith College Museum of Art. *Ill. p.126.*

FORBES, Donald. Born Auburn, Neb. 1905. Self-taught. Worked on New York WPA Art Project. Lives New York.

*90 Millstone. c. 1936. 26¼ x 36". WPA Art Program. *Ill. p.99.*

91 José. 1940. 19 x 15". Museum of Modern Art, Mrs. Simon Guggenheim Fund.

FULLER, George. 1822-84. Born Deerfield, Mass. Studied briefly with sculptor H. K. Brown, Albany. 3 years as itinerant portrait painter; studied in Boston. Lived in New York 12 years. 1859 trip to Europe. Little success with portraits or landscapes; 1860 retired to family farm in Deerfield, painting only in leisure time until 1876 when he exhibited in Boston with financial and artistic success. Studio in Boston. Died Brookline, Mass.

92 And She Was a Witch. 30 x 40". Lent by Metropolitan Museum of Art.

GRAVES, Morris. Born Fox Valley, Ore. 1910. Since 1911 lived chiefly in western Washington; high school in Beaumont, Tex. Trip to Japan, 1930; Puerto Rico, 1940. Worked on Washington WPA Art Project. Lives Anacortes, Wash.

GROPPER, William. Born New York 1897 of Lithuanian parentage. 1913-18 National Academy, New York School of Fine and Applied Art. Well-known graphic artist; cartoonist for *New York Herald Tribune* 1919; then for *Rebel Worker, Daily Worker, The Liberator, Vanity Fair, New Masses*. 1927 to Russia with Theodore Dreiser and Sinclair Lewis. Guggenheim fellowship 1937. Painter, illustrator, author. Section of Fine Arts murals, Detroit and Department of Interior, Washington. Lives Croton-on-Hudson, N. Y.

*97 The Defenders. 1941. 20 x 24". Lent by A.C.A. Gallery. *Ill. p.95.*

GROSZ, George. Born Berlin 1893. Studied at Dresden Academy and Kunstgewerbeschule, Berlin. 1913 to Paris. In German army 1914-18. Famous for satirical drawings of World War. Dadaist in Berlin, 1919. 1932 to U. S. Has taught at Art Students' League intermittently since 1932. Guggenheim fellowship 1937 and 1938. Lives Douglaston, Long Island.

98 Early Moon. 1939. 20 x 26". Lent by Associated American Artists.

*99 No Let-up. 1940. 29 x 21". Lent by Mr. and Mrs. Frederick B. Adams, Jr. *Ill. p.97.*

HALL, Carl. Born Washington, D. C. 1922. 1939-41 Meinzinger Art School, Detroit, under Carlos Lopez. Now in U. S. Army.

100 Interlochen, Michigan. 1940. 24¼ x 40". Lent by Museum of Fine Arts, Boston.

HART, "Pop" (George Overbury). 1868-1933. Born Cairo, Ill. Self-taught except for few months at Art Institute of Chicago and Julian Academy, Paris. From 1900 traveled and painted, doing odd jobs to pay his way, in Italy, Egypt, South Pacific islands, West Indies, Iceland, France. 1907 bought land and built shack, Coytesville, N. J.; painted signs for amusement parks and movie sets, Fort Lee, N. J. until 1920; from 1921 worked only at own painting. Trips to South America,

Mexico, North Africa, etc. Draftsman, print maker, watercolorist; recognition as artist after 1925. Died New York.

101 The Sultan's Messenger. 1929. Watercolor and pastel, 16⅜ x 22⅜″. Museum of Modern Art, given anonymously.

HARTLEY, Marsden. 1877-1943. Born Lewiston, Me. At 15, Cleveland School of Art; 1899 Chase School, New York; 4 years National Academy. Knew Ryder. 1908 work shown by Stieglitz at "291." To Europe 1912; 1914-16 France, Germany, exhibited Munich and Berlin with Kandinsky, Klee, Marc. 1918-20 Southwest U. S. 1921 to Europe, 4 years in Germany; 1926-27 France. Guggenheim fellowship 1930; to Mexico. From 1931, in New York and Maine. Worked on New York WPA Art Project. Published poems and essays. Died Ellsworth, Maine.

*102 Evening Storm, Schoodic, Maine. 1942. Oil on composition board, 30 x 40″. Museum of Modern Art, acquired through the Lillie P. Bliss Bequest. *Ill. p.93.*

HEADE, Martin Johnson. Active 1847-84. Born Bucks County, Pa. Began as portrait painter. Studied 2 years in Italy. To Brazil making sketches for proposed book on hummingbirds of South America. Studio in New York; worked also in Philadelphia, Trenton, St. Louis, Boston, Providence.

*103 Storm Approaching Larchmont Bay. 1868. 32⅛ x 54⅜″. Lent by Ernest Rosenfeld. *Ill. p.70.*

HOMER, Winslow. 1836-1910. Born Boston. Lithographer's apprentice, 1855. New York 1859; studied National Academy and with Frederic Rondel. Illustrations for *Harper's Weekly* and other periodicals 1858-76. War correspondent 1862-64. First oils, 1862. Paris 1867. Virginia, 1876-80. England, 1881-82. Settled at Prout's Neck, Maine, 1884; first of large marines. Subsequently visited Canada and the Adirondacks, the Bahamas, Cuba, Florida, Bermuda. Died Prout's Neck.

*104 The Gulf Stream. 1899. 30½ x 50¼″. Lent by Metropolitan Museum of Art. *Ill. p.79.*

HOPPER, Edward. Born Nyack, N. Y. 1882. 1900-05 Chase School under Henri and Hayes Miller. 1906-07 in Paris, influenced by Impressionism; 1909 and 1910 summers in Europe. Illustrator until 1924; known for etchings. 1924 successful show of watercolors; gave up commercial work and returned to oil painting. Lives New York.

105 Shakespeare at Dusk. 1935. 17 x 25″. Lent by Frank K. M. Rehn Gallery.

*106 Cape Cod Evening. 1939. 30 x 40″. Lent by Frank K. M. Rehn Gallery. *Ill. p.89.*

*107 Gas. 1940. 26¼ x 40¼″. Museum of Modern Art, Mrs. Simon Guggenheim Fund. *Color plate facing p.38.*

HULSART, Cornelius B., publisher, New York.

108 Capturing a Sperm Whale. 1835. Aquatint colored by hand; engraved by J. Hall; painted by William Page from sketch by C. B. Hulsart; 16¼ x 24¼″. Lent by Old Print Shop.

HUNT, William Morris. 1824-79. Born Brattleboro, Vt. 3 years at Harvard, then to Europe. Intended to become sculptor. Studied in Rome; c. 1844 in Paris with Barye; c. 1846 Düsseldorf where he disliked the teaching. Returned to Paris to take up painting. Favorite pupil of Couture c. 1847-52; then associated with Millet, living near him in Barbizon. Returned to America 1855, worked in Brattleboro and Newport, R. I.; from 1862 in Boston. Influential as teacher, patron, led trend away from Düsseldorf to French art. Murals in Albany State Capitol (later ruined). Drowned, Isles of Shoals, N. H.

109 The Jewess. Between 1847-52. 22 x 18½″ (oval). Lent anonymously, through Museum of Fine Arts, Boston.

*110 The Ball Players. 16 x 24″. Lent by Detroit Institute of Arts. *Ill. p.72.*

*111 The Bathers. 1877. 24 x 16″. Lent by Worcester Art Museum. *Ill. p.72.*

INMAN, Henry. 1801-46. Born Utica, N. Y. Apprenticed to Jarvis 7 years; traveled with him in U. S. Known for portraits, miniatures and genre paintings, although he preferred landscapes. Successful in New York and Philadelphia until 1838 when health failed. 1844 to England with commissions from friends to paint Wordsworth and others. Died New York.

112 A Picnic in the Catskills. 48 x 34⅛″. Lent by Brooklyn Museum.

INNESS, George. 1825-94. Born near Newburgh, N. Y.; family moved to Newark, N. J. Started as shopkeeper, then apprenticed to map engraver; turned to landscape painting. Brief study under Régis Gignoux, New York, but practically self-taught. 1847 to London and Rome for 15 months; to Paris early 1850s for 1 year, influenced by Barbizon. 1871 to Paris and Rome for 4 years. Lived last 15 years in Montclair, N. J. While traveling in Scotland, died at Bridge of Allan.

*113 The Monk. 1873. 38½ x 64½″. Lent by Stephen C. Clark. *Ill. p.75.*

*114 The Approaching Storm. c. 1880. 27½ x 42″. Lent by Addison Gallery of American Art. *Ill. p.75.*

JOHNSON, Eastman. 1824-1906. Born Lovell, Me. At 15 apprenticed to Boston lithographer. At 18 started drawing portraits; before 1846 was well established in Washington, D. C. 1846-49 Boston; portraits of Longfellow, his family and friends. 1849 to Düsseldorf to study, sharing studio with Leutze. Visited Paris and London; painted 3½ years at The Hague. 1855 to U. S. 1856-57 painted Indians and frontier life, Wisconsin. 1857 portraits in Cincinnati; 1859 in Washington; then settled in New York. Turned to genre; followed Union Army during Civil War, sketching. Trips to Fryeburg and Kennebunkport, Me., Catskills; from 1870 summers at Nantucket. From mid-1880s painted chiefly portraits. Died New York.

115 A Ride for Liberty—The Fugitive Slaves. c. 1862-63? Oil on academy board, 21¾ x 26¼″. Lent by Brooklyn Museum.

*116 Girl Picking Water Lilies. 1865. Oil on academy board, 18½ x 15¼″. Lent by Mr. and Mrs. I. M. Cohen. *Ill. p.71.*

*117 *Study for* The Wounded Drummer Boy. c. 1870? Oil on academy board, 26¼ x 21½″. Lent by Fine Arts Society of San Diego. *Ill. p.71.*

118 Sugaring Off (unfinished). c. 1865-71? 52⅜ x 96″. Lent by Curt Valentin.

KANTOR, Morris. Born Minsk, Russia 1896. To U. S. 1909. 1914 started as cartoonist. Studied with Homer Boss, Independent School, New York, 1916-17. Spare-time painter for many years, until 1927 to Paris for a year. Worked on WPA Art Project, New York. Lives New York and New City, N. Y.

*119 Haunted House. 1930. 37 x 33¼″. Lent by Art Institute of Chicago. *Ill. p.104.*

120 South Truro Church. 1934. 24¼ x 27″. Museum of Modern Art, gift of Mrs. John D. Rockefeller, Jr. (by exchange).

KARFIOL, Bernard. Born near Budapest of American parents, 1886. To U. S. as child. 1900 studied National Academy; 1901 Julian Academy, Paris; in France 5 years. Returned to U. S. 1906. Lives Irvington-on-Hudson, N. Y.

*121 Boy. 1924. 36 x 27″. Lent by Phillips Memorial Gallery. *Ill. p.112.*

KENSETT, John Frederick. 1818-72. Born Cheshire, Conn. Apprenticed to engraver, his uncle, Alfred Daggett; painted in leisure time. 1840 to Europe with Durand; 7 years in England, Germany, Switzerland, Italy. Sent home paintings which established reputation in U. S. Settled in New York by 1848; successful career. Trip West 1866. Died New York.

*122 Seashore. 1860. 18 x 30″. Lent by New York Public Library, Stuart Collection. *Ill. p.68.*

KENT, Rockwell. Born Tarrytown Heights, N. Y. 1882. Studied with Chase, Henri, Hayes Miller, Abbott Thayer. In Newfoundland 1914-15; Alaska 1918; southern France, Ireland; Greenland 3 years; Tierra del Fuego 1922. Painter, illustrator, print maker, author. Formerly President of United American Artists, C.I.O. Lives Ausable Forks, N. Y.

*123 Toilers of the Sea. 1907. 37½ x 44″. Lent by Lewisohn Collection. *Ill. p.88.*

KIRKLAND, Vance H. Born Conway, Ohio 1904. Studied Cleveland School of Art with H. G. Keller. Section of Fine Arts murals, Eureka, Kan., Sayre, Okla. Director, Kirkland School of Art, Denver.

124 A Misty Landscape. 1943. Watercolor, 29 x 41″. Lent by the artist.

KOPMAN, Benjamin. Born Vitebsk, Russia 1887. To New York at 17. 1905-09 National Academy. Worked on New York WPA Art Project. Lives Far Rockaway, Long Island.

*125 A Lynching. 1930. 29 x 47″. Lent by Mr. and Mrs. Bernard Reis. *Ill. p.95.*

KURZ and ALLISON, publishers, Chicago.

126 The Great Conemaugh-Valley Disaster, Flood and Fire at Johnstown, Pa. 1889. Color lithograph, 17½ x 25″. Lent by Old Print Shop.

LA FARGE, John. 1835-1910. Born New York. Studied law and architecture; at 22 turned to the arts. To Europe 1856; studied briefly with Couture, Paris; Munich, Dresden, London, influenced by Pre-Raphaelites. Worked with Hunt at Newport, R. I., who strongly influenced him. 1886 to Japan; later Samoa and other Pacific islands. Essayist, lecturer, connoisseur; murals, stained glass, mosaics, sculpture. Died Providence, R. I.

*127 Portrait of the Artist. 1859. Oil on wood, 16 x 11½″. Lent by Metropolitan Museum of Art. *Ill. p.73.*

*128 The Wolf Charmer. 1907. 80½ x 62½". Lent by Washington University, St. Louis, through City Art Museum of St. Louis. *Ill. p.80.*

LEBRUN, Rico. Born Naples, Italy 1900. Studied art in Naples. Italian Army, World War. To U. S. 1924 to establish branch of Naples stained glass factory in Springfield, Ill. To New York 1925. Guggenheim fellowships, 1935 and 1937. Taught Art Students' League; Chouinard Art Institute, Los Angeles; Sophie Newcomb College, New Orleans. Lives Westport, Conn.

*129 Migration to Nowhere. 1941. Gouache on board, 30 x 48". Lent by the artist. *Ill. p.122.*

130 Cicada. 1943. 35 x 40". Lent by the artist.

LEVI, Julian E. Born New York 1900. Studied Pennsylvania Academy. To Europe 1920; Italy, 4 years in France. Worked on New York WPA Art Project. 1943 artist-correspondent on U. S. Navy project. Lives New York.

*131 Buoys. 1939. 18 x 22". Lent by John L. Sexton. *Ill. p.113.*

LUDINS, Eugene David. Born Russia 1904. To New York as a child. Studied Art Students' League. Worked on New York WPA Art Project. Since 1930 has lived Woodstock, N. Y.

132 Rotten Foundations. 1938. 30⅛ x 50⅛". Lent by Associated American Artists.

*133 Interlude. 1940. 36½ x 48¾". Lent by Associated American Artists. *Ill. p.117.*

MacIVER, Loren. Born New York 1909. Studied Art Students' League, National Academy. Worked on New York WPA Art Project. Lives New York.

*134 The Violet Hour. 1943. 90½ x 57¾". Lent by Pierre Matisse Gallery. *Ill. p.127.*

MANGRAVITE, Peppino. Born Lipari Island, Italy 1896. To U. S. 1912; to live 1915. Studied Cooper Union 1915-16; Art Students' League 1917. Guggenheim fellowships 1932 and 1936. Section of Fine Arts murals, Department of Labor, Washington, Atlantic City, N. J., Flushing and Hempstead, N. Y. Taught Colorado Springs Fine Arts Center, Cooper Union, Sarah Lawrence College, etc. Lives New York.

135 The Abduction of a Beautiful Lady. 1935. Gouache, 17½ x 11½". Lent by Whitney Museum of American Art.

MARIN, John. Born Rutherford, N. J. 1870. Worked in architects' offices 4 years. Earliest watercolors 1888. 1899-1901 Pennsylvania Academy with Anshutz; 1901-03 Art Students' League, New York. 1905 to Europe for 4 years; lived in Paris; traveled Italy, Holland, Belgium, England. Etchings, oils, watercolors. 1909 first show at Stieglitz' gallery "291"; returned to U. S. 1910-11 to Europe again; Paris, Tyrol, Germany. In U. S. since 1911. Lives Cliffside, N. J. and Maine.

*136 Sunset, Casco Bay. 1919. Watercolor, 16 x 19½". Lent by Georgia O'Keeffe. *Ill. p.91.*

137 Lower Manhattan. 1920. Watercolor, 21⅞ x 26⅞". Lent by Philip L. Goodwin. Ill. *Art in Our Time*, no. 212.

138 On Morse Mountain, Small Point, Maine. 1928. Watercolor, 21 x 16½". Lent by Philip L. Goodwin. Ill. in color *John Marin*, facing p.22.

139 Storm Over Taos, New Mexico. 1930. Watercolor, 15¼ x 21". Lent by An American Place. Ill. *John Marin*, color frontispiece.

MATTSON, Henry Elis. Born Gothenburg, Sweden 1887. To U. S. 1906. Worked as mechanic, Worcester, Mass., studying at Art Museum. Largely self-taught. To Sweden to study art but returned to America; worked for International Harvester Co., Chicago. Guggenheim fellowship 1935. Section of Fine Arts mural, Portland, Me.; worked on New York WPA Art Project. Since 1916 has lived in Woodstock, N. Y.

140 Moonlit Still Life. 1938. 24 x 36". Ill. *Art in Our Time*, no. 129.

*141 Stars and Sea. 1941. 36 x 42". *Ill. p.108.*

*142 Jungle Play. 1941. 26 x 40". *Ill. p.109.*

143 Night Witchery. 1941. 16 x 24".

Nos. 140-43, lent by Frank K. M. Rehn Gallery.

MEEKER, Joseph Rusling. Born Newark, N. J. 1827. To New York 1845, studied National Academy. Painted 3 years in Buffalo; 1852-59 in Louisville, Ky., later, studio, St. Louis. Landscape, figure and portrait painter.

144 Lake Pontchartrain. 1876. 20⅛ x 36". Lent by Mrs. Leighton K. Montgomery.

MELCARTH, Edward. Born Louisville, Ky. 1914. Studied Chelsea Art School, London; Académie Ranson, Paris; with Karl Zerbe, Boston, 1935-36. 1942 to Iran as truck driver in construction work; now able-bodied seaman, Merchant Marine.

145 Girl's Head. 1943. 12 x 10". Lent by Durlacher Brothers.

MILLER, Alfred Jacob. 1810-74. Born Baltimore. Studied with Sully. Successful in Baltimore and Washington. To Europe 1833, studying in Paris, Florence, and Rome where he knew Thorwaldson, Greenough. 1837 in New Orleans met Scotsman, Sir William Drummond Stewart, who traveled with him to Rocky Mountains and commissioned series of Indian paintings now in Scotland. 1841 in Scotland, painting portraits. Returned Baltimore; painted portraits until his death there.

*146 Buffalo Hunt. c. 1840. 30 x 44". Lent by Victor D. Spark. *Ill. p.60.*

MILLMAN, Edward. Born Chicago 1907. Studied Art Institute of Chicago; fresco painting in Mexico. WPA murals, Chicago; Section of Fine Arts frescoes, Decatur and Moline, Ill., St. Louis. Lives New York. Now in U. S. Navy.

147 Two Ghosts. 1942. 24 x 30". Lent by the artist.

MOMMER, Paul. Born Duchy of Luxembourg 1899. Practically self-taught. In German army, World War; 2 years in England as prisoner-of-war. Merchant seaman 1920-21. To U. S. 1921. Has had various jobs; paints only in spare time. Worked on New York WPA Art Project. Lives New York.

148 The Betrayal. 1939. 30 x 40". Lent by the artist.

*149 At Night. 1940. 30 x 40". Lent by the artist. *Ill. p.109.*

MORAN, Thomas. 1837-1926. Born Lancashire, England. To America 1844. Wood engraver and illustrator in Philadelphia; turned to painting. Twice to Europe, influenced by Turner and Claude Lorraine. 1871 and 1873 accompanied government exploring expedition to Yellowstone region. Huge canvases of Western scenery very popular. Studio Easthampton, Long Island. Died Santa Barbara, Calif.

*150 Cliffs of the Upper Colorado River, Wyoming Territory. 1882. 15⅝ x 23½". Lent by National Collection of Fine Arts, Smithsonian Institution. *Ill. p.76.*

MORSE, Samuel Finley Breese. 1791-1872. Born Charlestown, Mass. Yale 1810. Pupil of Allston, accompanying him to England 1811; remained 4 years. Friend of Turner, Sir Thomas Lawrence, Coleridge, Wordsworth. 1815 returned to U. S.; painted portraits for a living with only moderate success. A founder of National Academy of Design, its first president 1827-45; also 1861-62. After 1832 devoted much time to his invention of the telegraph, eventually giving up painting. Introduced daguerreotype to America. Died New York.

151 The Greek Boy (Christos Evangelides). 1828. 21 x 17" (oval). Lent by M. Knoedler & Co.

*152 The Chapel of the Virgin at Subiaco. 1830-31. 30 x 37". Lent by Worcester Art Museum. *Ill. p.56.*

MOUNT, William Sidney. 1807-68. Born Setauket, Long Island, N. Y. About 1824 apprenticed to brother, a portrait and sign painter in New York; 1826 studied National Academy. 1829, studio in New York, portrait and genre painter. 1836 poor health caused return to Long Island. 1843 visited Cole at Catskill. Painted local farm and village life, designed horsedrawn "portable studio." Painted for Currier & Ives. Died East Setauket.

*153 Landscape with Figures. 1851. 19 x 28¼". Lent by Pennsylvania Academy of the Fine Arts. *Ill. p.64.*

NEWMAN, Robert Loftin. 1827-1912. Born Richmond, Va. 1838 family moved to Clarksville, Tenn. 1850 to Paris, studied with Couture; 1854 again to Paris; associated through Hunt with Millet at Barbizon. Returned to South to paint. Conscripted by Confederate Army in Civil War; 1865-66 worked way to New York, painting political banners in Baltimore. Lived rest of life in New York, occasional trips to Paris and London. Died New York.

154 Chrysanthemums. 29¾ x 25". Lent by Frank K. M. Rehn Gallery.

155 The Attack. 12 x 18". Lent by Frank K. M. Rehn Gallery.

*156 The Fortune Teller. 10 x 14". Lent by Metropolitan Museum of Art. *Ill. p.80.*

O'KEEFFE, Georgia. Born Sun Prairie, Wis. 1887. Studied Art Institute of Chicago; Art Students' League with Chase. Gave up painting; several years as advertising artist; then studied with Bement at University of Virginia, and with Dow at Teachers' College, New York. Head of art department, West Texas State Normal College 4 years; began to paint again. In 1916 collection of drawings exhibited by Alfred Stieglitz; gave up teaching to paint. Lives New York and New Mexico.

*157 Black Cross, New Mexico. 1929. 39 x 30". Lent by Art Institute of Chicago. *Ill. p.90.*

158 Ranchos Church No. 3. 1929. 15 x 11". Lent by An American Place.

159 Deer's Skull and Pedernal. 1936. 36 x 30". Lent by An American Place.

ORR, Elliot. Born Flushing, Long Island, N. Y. 1904. Studied with Luks; Grand Central Art School. Worked on Massachusetts WPA Art Project. Lives Waquoit, Mass. Now in U. S. Navy.

160 The Treasure. 1939. 12 x 10″. Lent by Kleemann Galleries.

161 The Dying Ship. 1941. 30 x 20⅛″. Lent by Kleemann Galleries.

*162 Desecration. 1941. 24 x 30″. Lent by Lt. and Mrs. Alastair Bradley-Martin. *Ill. p.110.*

OSVER, Arthur. Born Chicago 1912. Art Institute of Chicago traveling fellowship 1937. Worked on Illinois WPA Art Project. Lives New York.

*163 Melancholy of a Rooftop. 1942. 48 x 24″. Museum of Modern Art, Mrs. Simon Guggenheim Fund. *Ill. p.125.*

PAGE, William. 1811-85. Born Albany, N. Y. 1820 to New York; at 14 in law office; left to study briefly with the portrait painter, James Herring; then with Morse at National Academy. About 1828 decided to enter Presbyterian ministry; 2 years study at Andover and Amherst. 1830 returned to art; from 1835 recognized portrait painter. Worked in Boston and New York; 1849 to Europe, living mostly in Rome until return to New York 1860. Friend of Inness. 1866 settled in Tottenville, Staten Island, where he died.

164 Self-portrait. 1860. 59 x 36″. Lent by Detroit Institute of Arts.

*165 Portrait of Mrs. Page. c. 1860. 59 x 36¼″. Lent by Detroit Institute of Arts. *Ill. p.69.*

PALMER, William C. Born Des Moines, Iowa 1906. Studied Art Students' League with Hayes Miller, Boardman Robinson, Benton; fresco painting at Fontainebleau. Taught Art Students' League 4 years. WPA murals, New York; Section of Fine Arts murals, Post Office Department, Washington, Boston, Monticello, Iowa. Director, Munson-Williams-Proctor Institute School of Art, Utica, N. Y.

*166 Spring Landscape with Ruins. 1938. Tempera and oil on canvas, 24 x 30″. Lent by Midtown Galleries. *Ill. p.118.*

PELLEW, John C. Born Penzance, Cornwall, England 1903. At 14 apprenticed to firm of marine engineers; worked on patrol boats. To U. S. 1921. Sign painter until 1929. Lives Astoria, Long Island.

*167 East River Nocturne, No. 2. 1941. 28¼ x 36¼″. Lent by Contemporary Arts. *Ill. p.110.*

PICKENS, Alton. Born Seattle 1917. Studied about 6 months Portland Museum Art School. Came to New York 1939, where he now lives.

168 The Blue Doll. 1942. 42⅞ x 35″. Lent by the artist.

PITTMAN, Hobson. Born Tarboro, N. C. 1900. Studied Pennsylvania State College, Columbia University, Carnegie Institute. To Europe 1928, 1930 and 1935. Director of Art, Friends' School, Overbrook, Pa. Lives Upper Darby, Pa.

169 The Widow. 1937. 15 x 25″. Lent by Whitney Museum of American Art.

*170 Old Friends. 1941. 30⅛ x 40¼″. Lent by Philip L. Goodwin. *Ill. p.105.*

POLOS, Theodore C. Born Greece 1902. To U. S. at 14. Settled in the West 1922. Studied with Xavier Martinez, Spencer Mackay. Worked on California WPA Art Project. Lives San Francisco.

*171 Green Landscape. 1940. 16¼ x 20″. Lent by the artist. *Ill. p.96.*

PRICE, Clayton S. Born on a ranch, Iowa 1874. Until about 45, cowhand and ranchman, chiefly in Wyoming. Taught himself to draw animals on the range. At 31 spent 1 year at St. Louis School of Art. 1909-10 magazine illustrator, Portland, Ore. 1918 to San Francisco and Monterey to paint. 1929 to Portland to live. Worked on Oregon WPA Art Project.

*172 Fisherman. 1941. 34 x 42″. Lent by Detroit Institute of Arts. *Ill. p.94.*

QUIDOR, John. 1801-81. Born Tappan, N. Y. Studied briefly with Jarvis, New York. Unsuccessful as portrait painter, made living painting signs, coaches, fire engines. Preoccupied with literary sources, used themes from Irving and Cooper. Lived mostly in New York.

*173 The Money Diggers. 1832. 16¾ x 21½″. Lent by Mrs. Sheldon Keck. (From Irving *Tales of a Traveller.*) *Ill. p.58.*

174 Leatherstocking Meets the Law. 1832. 27¼ x 34¼″. Lent by New York State Historical Association. (From Cooper *The Pioneers.*)

REMINGTON, Frederic. 1861-1909. Born Canton, N. Y. Studied Yale School of Fine Arts, Art Students' League. Went West as cow-puncher. Magazine and book illustrator and writer, painter and sculptor of Western life, particularly Indians and cowboys. Illustrator of Theodore Roosevelt's books on West. Greatest popularity in '90s. Studio at New Rochelle, N. Y. Died near Ridgefield, Conn. Remington Art Memorial (museum), Ogdensburg, N. Y.

*175 Fired On. 26⅜ x 39¼″. Lent by National Collection of Fine Arts, Smithsonian Institution. *Ill. p.76.*

RICHARDSON, Constance Coleman. Born Berlin, Germany 1905, of American parents. Studied 3 years at Pennsylvania Academy. Lives Detroit.

176 Morning in the High Pasture. 1941. Oil on gesso, 20 x 26¼″. Lent by Macbeth Gallery.

RYDER, Albert Pinkham. 1847-1917. Born New Bedford, Mass. To New York with family about 1867. Studied briefly with William E. Marshall and 1871 National Academy of Design. To Europe 1893 with Daniel Cottier; England, Holland, Italy, Spain, Morocco. Exhibited National Academy 1873-88; Society of American Artists 1878-87; Armory Show 1913. Died Elmhurst, Long Island.

*177 Dead Bird. 1890-1900. Oil on wood, 4¼ x 9⅞″. Lent by Phillips Memorial Gallery, courtesy William Rockhill Nelson Gallery of Art, Kansas City. *Ill. p.84.*

*178 Macbeth and the Witches. 1890-1908. 28½ x 36″. Lent by Phillips Memorial Gallery. *Ill. p.82.*

*179 Moonlight—Marine. Oil on wood, 11⅜ x 12″. Lent by Metropolitan Museum of Art. *Ill. p.84.*

180 Elemental Forces. 21½ x 33½″. Lent by Addison Gallery of American Art.

181 The Forest of Arden. 19 x 15″. Lent by Stephen C. Clark. Ill. *Art in Our Time*, no. 28.

SARGENT, John Singer. 1856-1925. Born Florence, Italy, of American parents. As boy studied art, Italy, Germany, France. 1874 entered studio of Carolus Duran, Paris; 1879 studied Velasquez in Spain. 1881 turned definitely to portraiture. Successful in Paris until 1884, then to London. Lived mostly in London; many trips to America. During World War, official artist with British Expeditionary Forces in France. Died London.

*182 Robert Louis Stevenson. 1885. 20¼ x 24¼″. Lent by Mrs. Payne Whitney, through Metropolitan Museum of Art. *Ill. p.81.*

SIEVAN, Maurice. Born Gomel, Russia 1898. To U. S. 1907. Studied Pratt Institute, Educational Alliance, National Academy with Leon Kroll and Charles Hawthorne. Merchant seaman during World War. To Paris 1930-31, studied with André Lhôte. Worked on New York WPA Art Project. Lives Jamaica, Long Island.

183 Trees. 1943. 22 x 28″. Lent by Contemporary Arts.

SLOAN, John. Born Lock Haven, Pa. 1871; grew up in Philadelphia. At 16 supported family; studied at night with Anshutz at Pennsylvania Academy. Staff artist on *Philadelphia Press.* To New York 1905; magazine illustrator. One of "The Eight," who first exhibited in 1908. Helped organize Armory Show, 1913. Distinguished as etcher and painter of New York life. Taught Art Students' League 1914-31; its president 1931-32; president Society of Independent Artists since 1918. Section of Fine Arts mural, Yonkers, N. Y. Lives New York and Santa Fe, N. M.

*184 The City from Greenwich Village. 1922. 26 x 34″. Lent by Kraushaar Galleries. *Ill. p.88.*

SPARHAWK-JONES, Elizabeth. Born Baltimore, 1885. Studied 3 years with Chase at Pennsylvania Academy; won traveling scholarship. Lives Westtown, Pennsylvania.

185 New Hampshire, September 1938. 1938. Watercolor on canvas, 20¼ x 19½″. Lent by Frank K. M. Rehn Gallery.

*186 Lady Godiva. 1941. Watercolor on canvas, 20 x 24″. Lent by Mrs. Otto L. Spaeth. *Ill. p.121.*

SPENCER, Mrs. Lilly Martin. 1847-1902. Born England of French parentage. To America at 5; grew up in Cincinnati. Portrait and genre painter. Lived Newark, N. J. and New York, where she died.

*187 Reading. 1852. 50⅜ x 37⅞″. Lent by Victor D. Spark. *New title. Ill. p.64.*

SPRUCE, Everett Franklin. Born near Conway, Ark. 1907. Brought up on farm in Ozarks. Studied art Dallas, Texas 1926-29. Worked at Dallas Museum of Fine Arts 1930-40; assistant director from 1935. Since 1940 has taught College of Fine Arts, University of Texas. Lives Austin, Tex.

188 The Hawk. 1939. Oil on composition board, 19⅜ x 23½″. Museum of Modern Art, Purchase Fund. Ill. *Americans 1942*, p.121.

STUEMPFIG, Walter J. Born Germantown, Pa. 1914. Studied Pennsylvania Academy; 1934 traveling fellowship. Lives Collegeville, Pa.

189 Et Ego in Arcadia. 1943. 26 x 32". Lent by Durlacher Brothers.

*190 Dalliance at Cape May. 1943. 30 x 36". Lent by Durlacher Brothers. *Ill. p.124.*

THECLA, Julia. Born Illinois, of Scotch-Irish parentage. Has exhibited, watercolor annual, Art Institute of Chicago, since 1931. Worked on Illinois WPA Art Project. Lives Chicago.

*191 This. 1936. Pastel and watercolor, 19¼ x 14". Lent by David Porter. *Ill. p.128.*

192 Hand by the Sea. 1936. Pastel and watercolor, 12 x 12". Lent by David Porter.

THON, William. Born New York 1906. Self-taught except 1 month at Art Students' League. 1933 shipped with treasure-hunting expedition to Cocos Island, South America. Now in U. S. Navy.

193 The Brothers. 1943. 23¾ x 48⅛". Lent by Midtown Galleries.

TOBEY, Mark. Born Centerville, Wis. 1890. Self-taught. Lived in Chicago and New York; to Seattle 1923. Taught art 1931-38 at Dartington Hall, Totnes, South Devon, England. Worked on Washington WPA Art Project. Lives Seattle.

194 The Flow of the Night. 1943. Gouache on cardboard, 20¾ x 15½". Lent by the artist.

TRUMBULL, John. 1756-1843. Born Lebanon, Conn. Harvard 1773. Taught school, Lebanon; painted with homemade materials. Aide-de-camp to Washington in Revolutionary War. 1778 gave up army to study art. 1780 to Paris and London; worked in studio of Benjamin West. 1784 began series of historical canvases, including *The Declaration of Independence.* Numerous trips to England, carried out diplomatic missions for new American government. Finally settled in New York; 1816-25 president American Academy of Fine Arts. 1815 commissioned to decorate rotunda of Capitol in Washington; murals finished 1824, aroused criticism. 1831 turned over series of historical paintings to Yale University in exchange for annuity. Died New York.

*195 The Sortie from Gibraltar (2nd version). 1788. 20 x 30". Lent by Cincinnati Art Museum. *Ill. p.51.*

196 View of Niagara from below Great Cascade, on British Side. 24 x 36". Lent by Wadsworth Atheneum.

TWACHTMAN, John Henry. 1853-1902. Born Cincinnati, Ohio. Studied with Duveneck there; 1775 with Loefftz, Munich; with Boulanger and Lefebvre, Paris. Returned to U. S. 1885; settled near Greenwich, Conn. One of first Americans to experiment with Impressionist theories. Helped organize "Ten American Painters," 1898. Died Gloucester, Mass.

197 Landscape. 35 x 46⅛". Lent by Whitney Museum of American Art.

VANDERLYN, John. 1775-1852. Born Kingston, N. Y. Worked in New York print store, studied drawing at night. Aaron Burr became his patron, sent him to Philadelphia to study with Gilbert Stuart; 1796 financed trip abroad. In Paris 5 years, first American to study in France instead of England. 1803-15 lived and painted in England; in Rome with Allston, Paris for 7 years. Returned to U. S. 1815; exhibited nude, *Ariadne*, which caused uproar. Painted portraits, exhibited his panoramas of European cities, without much success. Died Kingston.

198 Death of Jane McCrea. 1803-05? 32½ x 26½". Lent by Wadsworth Atheneum.

VEDDER, Elihu. 1836-1923. Born New York. Studied in Paris and Italy. From 1867 lived in Rome and Capri, visiting and exhibiting in U. S. Illustrations, *Rubáiyát of Omar Khayyám*, 1884; murals, Library of Congress, Washington, in '90s. Died Rome.

*199 The Lair of the Sea Serpent. 1864. 21⅛ x 36⅛". Lent by Museum of Fine Arts, Boston. *Ill. p.69.*

WATKINS, Franklin Chenault. Born New York 1894. Has lived chiefly in Philadelphia. Studied University of Virginia, 1911-12; Pennsylvania Academy, 1916-17, 1920-21. In Europe 1921 on scholarship. Teaches Stella Elkins Tyler School of Fine Arts of Temple University, Philadelphia. Lives Germantown, Pa.

*200 Suicide in Costume. 1931. 36¼ x 44¼" (oval). Lent by Philadelphia Museum of Art. *Ill. p.120.*

*201 Soliloquy. 1932. 25 x 30". Lent by Whitney Museum of American Art. *Ill. p.121.*

202 Rocky Coast. 1933. 28 x 34". Lent by Miss Anna Warren Ingersoll.

WEBER, Max. Born Vialostok, Russia 1881. To America 1891; lived in Brooklyn. Studied 1897-1900 Pratt Institute with Dow. Taught art, 1900-05, public schools, Lynchburg, Va. To Paris 1905; Julian Academy with Laurens; knew Henri Rousseau, Picasso, Matisse, with whom he studied 1907. To Spain 1906; Italy 1907. Returned to New York 1909. Exhibition 1910 at Stieglitz' "291." Taught Art Students' League 1920-21, 1926. Author of essays and poems. Lives Great Neck, Long Island.

*203 Winter Twilight. 1940. 30 x 40". Lent by Mr. and Mrs. Buell Hammett. *Ill. p.92.*

*204 Chassidic Dance. 1940. 32 x 40". Lent by Mr. and Mrs. Milton Lowenthal. *Ill. p.92.*

WELLS, Cady H. Born Southbridge, Mass. 1904. Studied in Boston and with Andrew Dasburg, Taos, N. M. Lives Southbridge and Taos. Now in U. S. Army.

205 Summer Rains, Jacona. 1941. Watercolor, 22 x 29½". Lent by Addison Gallery of American Art.

WEST, Benjamin. 1738-1820. Born Springfield, Pa. of Quaker family. Went to Pennsylvania College; some art instruction in Philadelphia and New York, where he painted portraits. To Rome 1760 until 1763 when he went to London to live. Became foremost historical painter of his day in England; 1772 made historical painter to court of George III. Studio a popular center of teaching, especially for American artists. Charter member of Royal Academy; succeeded Sir Joshua Reynolds as its president, 1792 until death. Died London.

*206 Saul and the Witch of Endor. 1777. 20 x 26". Lent by Mrs. Frederic S. Gould. *Ill. p.50.*

*207 Death on the Pale Horse (study). 1802. 21 x 36". Lent by Philadelphia Museum of Art. *Ill. p.50.* (One of two extant studies for large canvas, 1817, Pennsylvania Academy of the Fine Arts.)

WHISTLER, James Abbott McNeill. 1834-1903. Born Lowell, Mass. 1843-49 in St. Petersburg, Russia, where father, a U. S. Army engineer, was supervising railroad construction. 1851 to West Point; dismissed end of 3rd year. 1855 to Paris; studied with Gleyre 2 years. 1859 settled in England. Influenced by Courbet, Manet, Degas, Fantin-Latour, Pre-Raphaelites, Velasquez. Early work followed French realists; 1860s interest in art of Far East; 1865 began "arrangements," "symphonies," "nocturnes." Whistler-Ruskin lawsuit 1878. To Venice 1879; Paris to live 1892; 1902 returned to London, where he died.

*208 Nocturne in Blue and Silver: The Lagoon, Venice. c. 1880. 20⅛ x 25⅞". Lent by Museum of Fine Arts, Boston. *Ill. p.73.*

WINTERS, Denny. Born Grand Rapids, Mich. 1909. Studied with Weisenborn; Chicago Academy of Fine Arts, Art Institute of Chicago. To California 1938. Worked on California WPA Art Project; also stage designing. Lives Los Angeles.

209 Wind in the Marshes. 1943. 26 x 34". Lent by the artist.

WYANT, Alexander Helwig, 1836-92. Born Port Washington, Ohio. Harness-maker's apprentice; painted signs. When about 20, saw paintings by Inness in Cincinnati, went East to seek Inness' advice. 1865 to study briefly in Karlsruhe, Germany, with Hans Gude; preferred works of Turner and Constable. Returned to New York. 1873 joined government expedition to Southwest; suffered paralytic stroke; learned to paint with left hand. Lived Arkville in Catskills. Died New York.

210 Moonlight and Frost. 28 x 36". Lent by Brooklyn Museum.

ZERBE, Karl. Born Berlin 1903. Studied at Munich Academy and in Italy, 1922-26. To U. S. 1934. Worked on Massachusetts WPA Art Project. Since 1937 head of Department of Painting, School of Museum of Fine Arts, Boston. Lives Cambridge, Mass.

*211 Terror. 1943. Encaustic on canvas, 29 x 36½". Lent by Downtown Gallery. *Ill. p.96.*

ARTISTS UNKNOWN

*212 Buffalo Hunter. 19th century. 40⅝ x 51½". Lent by Mr. and Mrs. Buell Hammett. *Ill. p.63.*

*213 Meditation by the Sea. 1860-65. 13¾ x 19½". Lent anonymously, through Museum of Fine Arts, Boston. *Ill. p.63.*

Index to Plates

Seven thousand five hundred copies of this book have been printed in November, 1943, for the Trustees of The Museum of Modern Art by The Plantin Press, New York. The color inserts have been printed by William E. Rudge's Sons, New York.

THIS REPRINTED EDITION WAS PRODUCED BY THE OFFSET PRINTING PROCESS. THE TEXT AND PLATES WERE PHOTOGRAPHED SEPARATELY FROM THE ORIGINAL VOLUME, AND THE PLATES RESCREENED. THE PAPER AND BINDING WERE SELECTED TO ENSURE THE LONG LIFE OF THIS LIBRARY GRADE EDITION.